WORSHIP

Also by Eric D. Huntsman

The Miracles of Jesus

God So Loved the World:
The Final Days of the Savior's Life

Good Tidings of Great Joy:
An Advent Celebration of the Savior's Birth

WORSHIP
Adding Depth to Your Devotion

ERIC D. HUNTSMAN

DESERET BOOK

Salt Lake City, Utah

© 2016 Eric D. Huntsman

All rights reserved. No part of this book may be reproduced in any form or by any means without permission in writing from the publisher, Deseret Book Company, at permissions@deseretbook.com or P. O. Box 30178, Salt Lake City, Utah 84130. This work is not an official publication of The Church of Jesus Christ of Latter-day Saints. The views expressed herein are the responsibility of the author and do not necessarily represent the position of the Church or of Deseret Book Company.

DESERET BOOK is a registered trademark of Deseret Book Company.

Visit us at DeseretBook.com

Library of Congress Cataloging-in-Publication Data
CIP data on file
ISBN 978-1-62972-098-2

Printed in the United States of America
Publishers Printing, Salt Lake City, UT

10 9 8 7 6 5 4 3 2 1

IN MEMORIAM
MARILYN HUNTSMAN (1938–2014)
optimae carissimaeque matris

To the best and dearest of mothers, who taught me to pray, prepared me for ordinances, shared the importance of the temple, instilled a love for holidays, read the scriptures with me, and gave me the gift of music.

In short, she taught me to worship.

CONTENTS

Preface ix
Acknowledgments xi
Introduction: What Is Worship? 1
1. Prayer 13
2. Ordinances and Other Rituals 34
3. Holy Places 55
4. Sacred Time 75
5. Reading, Preaching, and Teaching God's Word 94
6. Worshipping God through Music 112
   Conclusion: Making Worship More Meaningful 132
   Notes 139
   Sources 161
   Index 171

PREFACE

Like many people, I first learned about worship from my mother. When I was a small child, she taught me about God—that he was my Heavenly Father and that he loved me. Almost as soon as I could talk, Mother taught me that I could kneel, close my eyes, and talk to him as if he were there, and she promised that he would hear me. She and Dad took me to church, where I learned to sing hymns and take the sacrament. Later Dad baptized me, providing me with my first saving ordinance. In these ways, my parents taught me to worship. Now, as a father myself, I have had the great joy of teaching my own children what my parents taught me.

I learned more about worship as I grew older. My personal and professional study of history and the scriptures has deepened my understanding of it. My love of music and the temple has enriched it, and the practices and devotion of people of other faiths have encouraged me to participate in it more diligently. Still, I have found that if I am not careful, my worship can become rote, done out of habit or obligation. For worship to be powerful and transformative, we must be sincere and focused. Then it is accompanied more often with the Spirit, allowing us to feel that we are actually in the presence of the Lord.

PREFACE

In this book we will see how worshipping the Lord with all our heart, mind, and strength changes us, making us more like God and Jesus Christ. We will examine how people have worshipped the Lord in the scriptures and throughout history, drawing from these sources a better understanding of our practices as Latter-day Saints. Woven throughout the discussion are short vignettes or stories, including personal experiences, that illustrate how people, both within the Church and outside it, experience worship. Further, because the word of God has a great ability to draw us closer to the Lord, the text is leavened by a liberal use of scripture. Those passages of scripture that are also poetic have been formatted in verse to illustrate their literary as well as spiritual beauty. For similar reasons the lyrics of moving hymns have also been frequently included.

This book concludes with a few observations on how we can find renewed joy and inspiration as we deepen our devotion by doing better what we already do well, allowing worship to prepare us to return to the presence of our Father in Heaven.

ACKNOWLEDGMENTS

This book is dedicated to the memory of my mother, Marilyn Halversen Huntsman. Together she and Dad taught me to love and serve the Lord. I am grateful to them as well as to the family that Elaine and I are raising together. Although much of my devotion is private, my wife and children have helped me find greater joy and fulfillment in worship. My family inspires me, and both Elaine and my daughter, Rachel, read through the final version of the manuscript and made many helpful suggestions.

I have been blessed with good friends who have inspired me and stood as examples of devotion to God and the restored gospel of Jesus Christ. In particular, I am grateful to Andrew Unsworth, who shares with me a love for scripture, the temple, history, music, and traditional liturgy. Our conversations over the years have helped shape several important aspects of this book.

My former assistants Joshua Matson, Stuart Bevan, and especially Stephen Betts spent many hours helping me research and proofread early versions of the manuscript. My current team of assistants—Julia Min-tsu Chiou, Jacob Inman, and Brian Passantino—have been invaluable in gathering and checking sources. I appreciate each of them.

ACKNOWLEDGMENTS

I am thankful to my publisher, Deseret Book Company, for encouraging me and bringing this book to print. I owe particular recognition to my product director, Lisa Roper, and several reviewers for their helpful direction and guidance that made this book more accessible to a broader audience. Once again, I was fortunate to work with my long-time editor, Suzanne Brady, whose skill, attention, and wit made the sometimes difficult final stages of preparing a manuscript for publication a joy. I am also appreciative to Shauna Gibby, designer, and Malina Grigg, typographer.

Above all, I owe thanks to Almighty God and to my Savior, Jesus Christ. As I have striven to add depth to my own worship, I have felt their presence near.

Introduction

WHAT IS WORSHIP?
An Encounter with God That Inspires and Transforms the Worshipper

> *O come, let us worship and bow down:*
>   *let us kneel before the Lord our maker.*
> *For he is our God;*
>   *and we are the people of his pasture,*
>   *and the sheep of his hand.*
> *O worship the Lord in the beauty of holiness:*
>   *fear before him, all the earth.*
>   —Psalm 95:6–7; 96:9

As Latter-day Saints we worship as individuals, as families, and as a community, but although we understand many aspects of *how* we worship, we do not always consciously think about what worship is or what it is supposed to do for us. We assume that we are worshipping when we pray, go to church, take the sacrament, serve in the temple, sing hymns of praise, or care for others as Jesus would. But what makes a prayer different from simply reciting a list of things that we need or items for which we are grateful? How is participating in an ordinance different from simply going through the motions of a traditional ritual? What makes feasting upon the word of the Lord different from simply reading the scriptures? And what makes singing or playing beautiful music an act of praise? Because our words and actions are all that appear above the surface, how can we add true depth to our devotion?

We can readily list many of the different ways we worship, but actually defining *worship* often proves elusive. Still, as we talk about our experiences, we can at least describe how we *feel* when we worship. Most of us experience the Spirit most strongly when we truly turn to the Lord in times of great need, gratitude, sorrow, or joy. On the other hand, if we are not careful, our most familiar acts of worship can easily become rote, done out of habit or obligation. Sometimes our minds wander and our focus on the Lord fades. In this day and age, however, we can hardly afford to be casual in our worship. In a world that is increasingly challenging and even dangerous, and in a time when faith is questioned and often undermined, developing a strong and personal relationship with God and bringing his power into our lives is more essential than ever.

The English word *worship* originally meant valuing something greatly, or feeling love, awe, and respect for someone better and more powerful than ourselves.[1] People seem to have an innate drive to worship, and even those who are not formally religious are often deeply committed to some belief, philosophy, or system that gives meaning and structure to their lives.[2]

Adoration is another word that helps us understand what worship is because it combines the feelings of awe, veneration, and love that we feel for God when we sense his greatness or recognize his goodness to us.[3] In every dispensation, God has commanded his children to worship him. For instance, the first commandment Adam and Eve received after their expulsion from the Garden of Eden was that they call upon and worship the Lord their God, *loving* and *serving* him alone (Moses 5:4–5; D&C 20:19). Worship is thus equated with both *how we feel* about God and *what we do* for him.

Still, does God really need our praise and devotion, or has he commanded us to worship him because it somehow changes *us* for the better? Bringing about our immortality and eternal life is the Lord's work and glory (Moses 1:39). Everything he commands us to do, including commanding us to worship him, is meant to help us become more like him so that we can be reunited with him and Jesus Christ eternally (John 14:2–3; D&C 132:20–23).

Worship may best be understood as an actual encounter with God, whose most important purpose is to change *us*.[4] This transformation can happen, however, only when we worship in and through the name of Jesus Christ, worshipping as he has taught us and allowing his grace to sanctify and empower us. Truly worshipping requires that we deepen our devotion, worshipping with our heart, mind, and strength and striving to make the experience even more powerful by making the effort to prepare before, focus during, and be more aware after we worship.

Worshipping with Heart, Mind, and Strength

Worship may be hard to define and is not much easier to describe, but most of us know what it is when we experience it. Sometimes we glimpse what worship is when we find God reflected in the beauty of nature, a spiritual service, the face of a loved one, the line of a poem, or the strains of an enchanting song. In those moments we yearn to be with him. That happened to me one Sunday morning during a performance of Mack Wilberg's poignant and haunting arrangement of the American folk hymn "His Voice as the Sound of a Dulcimer Sweet."[5]

> *His voice as the sound of a dulcimer sweet,*
> *Is heard through the shadows of death;*
> *The cedars of Lebanon bow at his feet,*
> *The air is perfumed with his breath.*
>
> *His lips as a fountain of righteousness flow,*
> *That waters the garden of grace;*
> *From which their salvation the Gentiles shall know,*
> *And bask in the smile of his face.*
>
> *Love sits in his eye-lids and scatters delight*
> *Through all the bright mansions on high;*
> *Their faces the cherubim veil in his sight,*
> *And tremble with fullness of joy.*
>
> *He looks, and ten thousand of angels rejoice,*
> *And myriads wait for his word;*

> *He speaks—and eternity, filled with his voice,*
> *Re-echoes the praise of her Lord.*[6]

The image of trees bowing, nations rejoicing, and cherubim trembling before God moved me deeply as we sang. I realized that worship is not just something we understand with our minds: it is something we feel and experience. As the words and music flowed around me, I was uplifted and felt close to the Lord. In that moment, I felt that I had joined in true worship.

Moses taught, "Hear, O Israel: The Lord our God is one Lord: and thou shalt love the Lord thy God with all thine heart, and with all thy soul, and with all thy might" (Deuteronomy 6:4–5).[7] During his mortal ministry, Jesus reaffirmed this obligation to serve God with our heart, mind, and strength (Mark 12:29–30; parallels Matthew 22:37–38; Luke 10:27). The Lord repeated this commandment yet again at the opening of our own dispensation, declaring through Joseph Smith, "Wherefore, I give unto them a commandment, saying thus: Thou shalt love the Lord thy God with all thy *heart*, with all thy might, *mind*, and *strength;* and in the name of Jesus Christ thou shalt serve him" (D&C 59:5; emphasis added). These passages and others like them underscore the truth that loving and serving the Lord with all our hearts, minds, and strength are keys to worshipping in a way that will transform us.

How we display reverence and love for God reflects *how we feel about him* and is an important way of worshipping him with our *hearts.* The most common biblical words for *worship* (Hebrew, *ḥwh* or *šḥh;* Greek, *proskyneō*) mean prostration, literally bowing down before God to show submission, adoration, and loyalty.[8] Other ways of worshipping include standing respectfully, stretching out one's hands in supplication, crying aloud in joy or need, and whispering quietly in deference. What is essential among these various outward expressions are the inner feelings of respect and reverence that these physical acts represent. Today, in an age and culture far removed from those of the Old Testament and even the New Testament, we may show how we feel about God by closing our eyes and kneeling or bowing our heads as we pray; performing an ordinance with exactness or participating in it with reverence; speaking and acting respectfully in places where God is worshipped; keeping the Sabbath holy and celebrating Christ-centered holidays; listening attentively as his word is read or preached; and singing hymns with a joyful spirit.

How we speak to God shows and shapes *what we think about him* and represents worshipping with our *minds*. Words and thoughts of worship—expressions of praise, love, need, gratitude, and faith—demonstrate that we love God, and the language we use influences the way we think and feel. But worshipping God with our minds is not only about words. Some acts of worship, such as the gestures included in an ordinance, carry great symbolism, sometimes meaning more than words alone. As a result, such actions can influence us even when we perform them silently. Ideally, worship should not consist of rote phrases or actions that are repeated without thought: the repeated phrases and set performances of an ordinance should be meaningful because of what they represent. Because worshipful words and acts influence how we think and feel, they are important means of our becoming more like God.

While serving the Lord with all our strength certainly includes the focus and intensity of our worship, what may be even more significant is how worship inspires us and enables us to serve him afterwards. As a result, *how we act because we have worshipped* is an important way of loving God with all our *strength*. President Dieter F. Uchtdorf, second counselor in the First Presidency, taught, "We obey the commandments of God—out of love for Him! Trying to understand God's gift of grace with all our heart and mind gives us all the more reasons to love and obey our Heavenly Father with meekness and gratitude."[9] Jesus taught at the Last Supper, "If ye love me, keep my commandments" (John 14:15) and "as I have loved you . . . love one another" (John 13:34). In short, worship of God is best evidenced in how we live and in how we treat others. When we feel God's Spirit and presence in our lives, we should be transformed and led to *feel, think,* and *act* differently as a result.

Creating Space for Worship

One Friday evening during a visit to Jerusalem, my daughter and I took my sister's husband to the Western Wall so we could witness how our Jewish friends welcomed the Sabbath at their most holy site. While my brother-in-law and I went up to the wall in the area reserved for men, my daughter, Rachel, went alone to the women's section. Later I returned to the partition that separated the men's and women's areas to wait for her.

As I stood there, I noticed an elderly Jewish woman standing towards the rear of the women's section, worshipping alone in the back while most of the other women were pressing towards the front near the wall. I was struck by the intensity of this woman's personal devotions. With her *siddur,* or prayer book, in one hand, she reached heavenward with the other as she joyfully called upon the Lord. Then, in the next instant, with that same hand she beat her breast as she turned her face downward and rocked in seeming sorrow. Despite all the crowds about her, she was alone with her God in that moment, having created her own space for worship. Although aware that I was observing a very private moment, I could not turn away. I was deeply moved by how fully she was sharing the full breadth of her thoughts and feelings with the Lord. She was truly in the presence of holiness.

As Latter-day Saints we worship the Father in the name of the Son by the power of the Spirit,[10] though certainly our feelings of love, reverence, and devotion extend to Jesus Christ and to the Holy Ghost as well.[11] Because the fall of Adam and Eve, our own mortal birth, and subsequent transgressions have separated us from God, both physically and spiritually,[12] in this life we must experience God through revelation. President Boyd K. Packer (1924–2015), long a member of the Quorum of the Twelve Apostles and president of that council from 2008 to 2015, taught that such revelation requires reverence, or proper feelings for God.[13]

As a result, one of the most important things we can do to prepare for worship is to foster the reverence that is conducive to feeling his Spirit. I have found that this often means we must step away from the world and its concerns so that we can actively create space for worship. There are, of course, specific places and times that are powerful venues and occasions for worship, but because we are to be witnesses of God "at all times and in all things, and in all places" (Mosiah 18:9), we can and should worship God anytime, anywhere. Whether sitting in the celestial room of the temple, kneeling by our beds, driving our cars, or walking in the press of a busy street, like the elderly Jewish woman whom I saw praying at the Western Wall, we must actively make room for the Spirit.

To do so, we must first make mental and spiritual space by focusing on the Lord, recognizing his goodness, and opening our hearts to him. Creating space for worship may require taking more time and making more effort than usual to prepare: clearing our minds and actively seeking the Spirit before we pray, participate in an ordinance, read our scriptures, or sing. Preparing also includes doing such simple things as arriving early for sacrament meeting or a temple session and listening to the prelude music.

The common factor in preparing for worship is seeking the feelings of reverence that the scriptures describe as "the fear of the Lord" (Isaiah 11:2; parallel 2 Nephi 21:2; Proverbs 9:10). The biblical words for *fear* (Hebrew, *yārē'*; Greek, *phobeomai*) included feeling profound respect, wonder, and amazement, or what might be best described as "being in awe."[14] Feeling reverence not only prepares us for worship but also invites the Spirit, which helps us feel God's presence as we worship.

Focus and Intentionality

When I was four years old, my family lived in Albuquerque, New Mexico. In those days we had Primary, Mutual, and Relief Society meetings on weeknights and went to church two different times on Sunday. Priesthood and Sunday School classes were held in the mornings, and we went back later in the day for sacrament meeting. This gave us the opportunity of receiving the sacrament twice each Sunday, once in the opening exercises of Sunday School and later that evening in sacrament meeting itself.

In the mornings children under twelve met separately in what was called Junior Sunday School. It was up to our teachers to keep rows of fidgety young children reverent, not only in class but when the sacrament was blessed and passed to us. In class after one not very reverent opening exercise, my Junior Sunday School teacher tried to help her young charges better understand why the sacrament was important and why we should be more reverent as it was administered.

I do not even remember this good sister's name, but what she taught me, as a small boy, that morning changed the way that I have experienced that sacred ordinance ever since. After reading from one of the Gospels the story of the Last Supper, she told us what she did to feel the Spirit during the administration of the sacrament. With some emotion, she explained that after the sacrament hymn was sung and during the blessing and passing of the bread and water, she tried to picture in her mind each of the things that Jesus did for her in those last hours of his life—his suffering in the Garden of Gethsemane, his betrayal, how he was mistreated and falsely judged, and how he had died upon the cross. Forty-six years later, I still remember what my teacher taught me, and I have tried to follow her example ever since. When I do, taking the sacrament becomes true worship.

Without a sincere attitude and proper intent, we might find ourselves simply going through the motions of worship. Once we have created space for worship, focusing on what we are doing and trying to imagine that we are in the presence of the Lord are necessary as we participate in an ordinance, pray, read, or sing. In the Jewish tradition, this kind of focus is called *kavanah*. Coming from a Hebrew word meaning "to direct," *kavanah* means directing the heart and mind towards God.[15] Rabbi Hayim Donin described *kavanah* as "to transform reading into prayer, there must be at least a sense of standing in the presence of God and the intent to fulfill one of His commandments."[16]

We, too, need *kavanah,* or proper intent, for any of our acts of worship to be true worship, and then we need to maintain that focus as we worship. Participating in ordinances, such as partaking of the sacrament, and other forms of worship can become rote acts if we do not really think about them. Our personal prayers may not escape the confines of our bedroom and our public prayers may be nothing but speeches in front of our class or ward if we do not sense that we are actually addressing God. Singing hymns is just singing if our singing of those sacred songs is not truly praising God or testifying and teaching of his truths.

The concept of intentionality is an important part of such focus in worship. Intentionality includes doing something with real intent, but it means more than that. Originally, the word *intend* meant to stretch or reach for something,[17] and in philosophy and linguistics, *intentionality* refers to the mind's ability to form an understanding or representation of something before acting.[18] In other words, we need to be able to conceive of something before we can do it. As a result, I suggest that we can use intentionality to help us understand the importance of having both a clear purpose *and* a firm awareness of God's presence or his Spirit as we worship. When we worship with such purpose and awareness, imagining that we are truly coming before the Lord, our worship becomes a way of reaching out to him. After a powerful encounter with God, Abraham said, "Thy servant has sought thee earnestly; now I have found thee" (Abraham 2:12). For us as well, finding the Lord is the first and greatest goal of our worship.

Mindfulness and Transformation

Midway through my junior year of high school, a change in my father's job led my family to relocate from the greater Pittsburgh area of Pennsylvania to a mid-sized town in western Tennessee. It was difficult as a teenager to move under any circumstances, but leaving friends and happy school activities to go to a place where I didn't know anyone was particularly hard. The change was aggravated by culture shock as we moved from a casually religious area in the northeastern United States to a small town in the solidly evangelical southern Bible Belt.

I was in a somewhat rebellious phase of life anyway, so I held my parents responsible for most of my unhappiness. Several mornings, feeling surly, I refused to join them for family prayer. My parents were already worried about me, and I knew that things I had been saying and doing were breaking my dear mother's heart.

On one of those mornings, as I hurried to leave for school, I passed my parents' partly opened bedroom door and glimpsed them kneeling by their bed. Dad was leading their prayer, and although I cannot remember now much of what he said, I knew that he and Mom were praying for me. I felt that I was witnessing something special, something sacred. In the course of those few moments, I sensed their concern and sadness change to hope, reassurance, and new purpose as they prayed to know what to do for me. But the change that occurred as two parents prayed for their son did not happen only in them. In that moment I felt the Spirit as I shared in their worship, even from outside their door, and my heart was softened.

When we feel the Spirit, that feeling changes us, but recognizing and appreciating this transformation requires that we be aware of it. Although these changes can be dramatic, as with conversion, sometimes they are subtler, consisting of comfort, peace of conscience, gentle promptings, or renewed strength and resolve to do the Lord's will. To experience them fully, we must be mindful both as we worship and also afterwards. Such mindfulness includes not only making sure we know what we are doing and why we are doing it but also being aware of how the experience has affected us.[19] We cannot and should not try to dictate how and when we will feel the Spirit or how God will answer our prayers. The Lord reveals himself to us "in his own time, and in his own way, and according to his own will" (D&C 88:68). That sometimes requires us to wait upon him (Psalm 27:14). As a result, mindfulness in worship also includes acceptance, and that kind of submission can be the greatest transformation we could hope for, because it means truly following Jesus' example of obedience and selflessness.

We may wonder whether we feel the Spirit because we are worshipping or whether having feelings of love and awe for God leads us to worship. The reality is that it can be either or both. At times we are drawn to worship because of the gratitude or love we feel for God. Other times we worship out of duty, and in the process the Spirit comes upon us in greater measure. Regardless of which comes first, ideally the two build upon each other in crescendo: the more we express our love and gratitude for God, the more we feel his Spirit, which leads us to serve him more fully, causing him to become more real to us as his Spirit becomes more palpable about us. But rarely does this cycle work if we merely go through the motions of worship. Instead, when we actively invite the Spirit, we can experience a greater measure of the Lord's power, goodness, and glory, bringing us into the presence of holiness.[20]

Loving God completely—including being in utter awe of him and the grace he gives us through his Son Jesus Christ—changes us. Indeed, for Christians, especially Latter-day Saints, true worship takes place in and through Jesus Christ, who shares his saving, empowering, and transforming Spirit with us. This transformation helps bring about forgiveness of our sins, it changes our hearts and minds, and it inspires us and empowers us to keep his commandments. Ultimately it exalts us. That is how we, "by a godly walk and conversation," show God and ourselves that we are "walking in holiness before the Lord" (D&C 20:69).[21] Indeed, feeling his Spirit and tasting of his holiness gives us the strength and means to serve his other children and to become more like him.

The Different Ways We Worship

In July 1985, Krister Stendahl, the Lutheran bishop of Stockholm, held a press conference to address mounting opposition to the Latter-day Saint temple being built in that city. At that briefing, Bishop Stendahl, one-time dean of the Harvard Divinity School, proposed three rules of religious understanding. These included advising individuals to ask adherents rather than opponents about a religion; refraining from comparing your best with their worst; and leaving room for "holy envy," by which he meant being willing to see beauty in another tradition that you would like to see in your own religious community.[22]

Bishop Stendahl's willingness to be inspired by Latter-day Saint temple building and theology has encouraged me to be similarly moved by the worship practices of others. Long impressed by the devotion of my Catholic friends when I was growing up in Pittsburgh and later by the devotion of my evangelical friends in Tennessee, I was able to extend the principle of holy envy further while I lived and taught at the Brigham Young University–Jerusalem Center in 2011 and 2012. As I witnessed the intensity and commitment of the various Jewish, Christian, and Muslim communities in the Holy Land, I resolved to be more genuine and intentional in my own worship.

We will proceed with the understanding that worship is an encounter with God that transforms us as worshippers, sanctifying us and empowering us to better serve him and his children. Although it is not possible to consider every way we can experience God and be changed by him, in the chapters that follow we will consider how we worship through prayer, ordinances, holy places, sacred time, the word of God, and uplifting music. Each chapter begins by reviewing some of the scriptural and historical precedents for these types of worship. Indeed, considering Bishop Stendahl's proposition concerning holy envy, or seeing the beauty in other traditions, allows us to be inspired and encouraged in our own worship by the commitment and devotion of others, even if we do not necessarily embrace their specific practices. Each chapter culminates by reviewing Restoration contributions to each form of worship and considers how we worship as individuals, as families, and as a church today.

With all these forms of worship, we emphasize the importance of worshipping with our hearts, minds, and strength while considering how preparation before, focus during, and awareness after our worship can deepen our experience and make our worship more powerful. We prepare ourselves for worship by creating space—physically, temporally, mentally, and spiritually—to meet the Lord. We focus with intentionality, meaning with proper intent and an awareness that we are truly reaching for God and experiencing his Spirit. Finally, we allow our worship to change us when we are mindful—stepping back, allowing ourselves to be conscious of God and his Spirit, and sensing how *he* is striving to change *us*.

Finally, we conclude with some brief suggestions about how we might find renewed joy and inspiration as we seek to deepen our devotion and make our own worship more meaningful by doing better what we already do well. Such worship not only transforms us but also moves us to love and serve others, becoming more like the Savior in the process. Worship then prepares us for a far greater future transformation as we follow the course to eternal life set for us by Jesus Christ, our Savior.

1

PRAYER

Communing with God and Feeling His Spirit

> *As for me, I will call upon God;*
> *and the Lord shall save me.*
> *Evening, and morning, and at noon,*
> *will I pray, and cry aloud:*
> *and he shall hear my voice.*
> *—Psalm 55:16–17*

As young children, often as soon as we are able to speak, most of us learn how to pray. From that point on, of all the ways we worship, prayer is the most regular way we seek to encounter God, communicating directly with our Father in Heaven and feeling his Spirit. People in every age and almost every known culture have engaged in some form of prayer.[1] As Latter-day Saints we pray as individuals, as families, and in groups. Some of our prayers are public; others are the most private, intimate conversations possible, occurring only in our minds and hearts. "To pray" originally meant "to request, entreat, beg, or ask earnestly,"[2] but prayer is more than just a means of asking for something. President Henry B. Eyring of the First Presidency taught that God the Father "offers us, through prayer in the name of His Son, *the opportunity to commune with Him in this life* as often as we choose."[3] This idea of communing makes prayer more than just an attempt to talk to God while we are not physically in his presence. It suggests real interaction between us and God, both receiving answers from him in response to our prayers and also exchanging real feelings with him. We not only share our worries, concerns, needs, joys, gratitude, and hopes with him in prayer but also feel his love in return and strive to listen as he speaks to us.

Because we usually think of our prayers as consisting of words and thoughts, praying is first of all a way of worshipping the Lord with our minds. But without preparation and focus, we can find ourselves talking *to* God—or, even worse, simply talking *at* God—rather than speaking *with* him. Taking time to prepare, even if for only a few seconds, allows us to create a space for worship that allows us to be aware that we are actually engaging with God. We must then exercise faith as we pray, believing that he is hearing us and reaching back to us as we pray. This kind of intentional focus is what the Jewish tradition calls *kavanah*. Without concentration, focus, and purpose, our prayers can be mere words or wishes, which explains why we sometimes need to spend as much time preparing to pray as we do actually praying.[4]

Prayer can be more than communing. Abraham Millgram (1900–1998), a noted Jewish educator, observed, "Prayer is born of man's sense of wonder, from his awareness of God's marvelous creation and the miracles that daily bear witness of God's goodness and love."[5] As a way of serving the Lord with our hearts, prayer includes cultivating a sense of awe and love for God, which we often express by the reverence we show and feel as we pray. Praying with our hearts also means fully sharing all our feelings with him, even those that we cannot easily articulate. In his well-known hymn "Prayer Is the Soul's Sincere Desire," James Montgomery (1771–1854) expressed the often wordless aspects of prayer:

> *Prayer is the soul's sincere desire,*
> *Uttered or unexpressed,*
> *The motion of a hidden fire*
> *That trembles in the breast.*
>
> *Prayer is the burden of a sigh,*
> *The falling of a tear,*
> *The upward glancing of an eye*
> *When none but God is near.*[6]

In response to a heartfelt, pained prayer, the Lord told Joseph Smith, "Be still and know that I am God" (D&C 101:16; see also Psalm 46:10). Being still can also be a form of prayer, as we wait upon the Lord, meditate, or just enjoy feeling his Spirit. Remembering that God is above all a loving Parent, we can allow ourselves to be "encircled about eternally in the arms of his love" (2 Nephi 1:15). These too are important ways of communing with God.

Sometimes overlooked, but equally important, is what we do *after* we pray. Being mindful means waiting for God to answer, listening to him, and then allowing him to change our hearts, inspire us, and empower us to act. The Danish philosopher and Christian Existentialist Søren Kierkegaard (1813–1855) famously observed that "the function of prayer is not to influence God, but rather to change the nature of the one who prays."[7] After encountering the Lord in prayer, we must then go forward and do something. When this happens, prayer is a way of worshipping the Lord with all our strength.

As we consider what the scriptures teach us about prayer and reflect upon some of the practices of other believers, we can ask ourselves what we can do to make our own prayers more meaningful. What role does reverence and showing our love for God play in helping us prepare to actually speak with him? How can we better focus so that we feel that we are actually in his presence as we pray? In what ways can we better feel God's Spirit and direction during and after prayer so that praying can change us and help us better serve him? Restoration scripture and teaching provide us important answers to many of these questions, but above all they stress the literal relationship that we have with God, transforming our prayers into heartfelt encounters between Parent and child.

Learning from Prayer in the Old Testament

Hayim Halevy Donin was a professor of Judaic Studies at the University of Detroit and the rabbi of the nearby Congregation B'nai David for twenty years. A prolific author, Rabbi Donin wrote about Jewish law, practice, and life. In the introduction of his book *To Pray as a Jew,* he shared a personal experience about the meaning—and experience—of prayer in his own life:

"I remember when as a young boy I watched my father, of blessed memory, recite his prayers. Sometimes, particularly on the High Holy Days, tears flowed from his eyes. I remember feeling embarrassed. I did not understand what made him cry. I wanted him to stop. I looked away. I still do not know what his thoughts were at those times, but now I understand. I was watching a most intimate communication between him and his Maker."[8]

As we seek to better prepare for prayer, recalling how people anciently tried to show reverence for God helps us consider how we can worship with our hearts as we pray. In Old Testament times prayer was often preceded by bowing down before the Lord. Prayers were then offered standing or kneeling in reverence, with worshippers often stretching their hands heavenward as they praised God or pleaded for blessings.[9] Elder Bruce R. McConkie (1915–1985), a long-time member of the Quorum of the Twelve Apostles and a prolific author, taught, "Any act of obeisance that gets us into the proper frame of mind when we pray is all to the good . . . almost by instinct, therefore, we do such things as bow our heads, close our eyes, fold our arms, or kneel, or fall on our faces."[10] Yet such outward actions are less important than what they represent. Creating space for worship means recognizing that we are turning from the here and now and entering the presence of our heavenly king, but inward feelings of love, gratitude, and awe that bring his Spirit are the most vital. For me, pausing, even for just a few moments, to remember who the Lord is, how much he loves me, and that he wants to help and bless me is as important as bowing my head and closing my eyes.

The scripture that recounts how the Lord spoke unto Moses "face to face, as a man speaketh unto his friend" (Exodus 33:11) speaks of the importance of intentionality during prayer. Although the Fall separated us as mortals from God's physical presence, Adam and Eve had earlier walked and talked with God in the Garden of Eden,[11] and that kind of fellowship is what true worship seeks to recreate. Examples ranging from Noah to Jeremiah portray prayer as real, two-way conversations,[12] which can help us picture ourselves actually standing or kneeling before God as we speak. What is important is that when we feel the Spirit as we pray, we *are* in his presence in an important sense, and that awareness should change the way we speak and feel as we pray.

Feeling that we are in the presence of a loving and powerful God also increases our desire to pray. This is why Old Testament passages encouraged praying morning, midday, and evening in order to think of God before, during, and after all of the day's activities (Psalm 55:17; Daniel 6:10). Such prayer was so important to Daniel, in fact, that he was willing to risk death in order to have those regular opportunities to feel the presence of the Lord. While we are generally encouraged to pray at least twice a day, usually upon awaking in the morning and then at night before bed, I have found that making time for at least one additional personal prayer helps me feel close to the Lord in the middle of the day, as it requires me to take a break from what I am doing and create space for worship by finding a time and a place to pray.

The Old Testament Psalms reflect a particularly rich diversity of prayers that remind us of the many things for which we can and should pray. These range from expressions of thanksgiving, petitions or requests, confessions and repentance, complaints, and even prayers that God will curse one's enemies.[13] This variety in the Psalms is so great because prayer is the most intimate form of communication, when we can and should be the most honest with the Lord, even when our feelings are less than positive. Above all else, the Psalms preserve powerful, poetic expressions of praise that can remind us of the importance of gratitude in prayer, which is particularly important because often our prayers can become occupied with things that we need and want. I often find that reading from this collection, whether aloud or silently, is a powerful way of creating sacred space for worship, helping me step back from the world and focus more on the Lord and his goodness before I begin to pray.

One of my favorite examples of prayer from the Old Testament is not that of a patriarch or a prophet but of a heartbroken woman. Suffering because of her barrenness, Hannah prepared herself to seek the Lord by fasting and going to the tabernacle at Shiloh, where she could find space for worship near God's presence. She then wordlessly poured out her heart to the Lord: "She was in bitterness of soul, and prayed unto the Lord, and wept sore. And she vowed a vow, and said, O Lord of hosts, if thou wilt indeed look on the affliction of thine handmaid, and remember me, and not forget thine handmaid, but wilt give unto thine handmaid a man child, then I will give him unto the Lord all the days of his life. . . . Now Hannah, she spake in her heart; only her lips moved, but her voice was not heard" (1 Samuel 1:10–13).

Hannah's silent prayer was indeed answered, and she conceived and gave birth to the future prophet Samuel. In gratitude, she offered a beautiful prayer of thanks (1 Samuel 2:1–10) and later dedicated her son to the Lord's service as she had promised. Because Hannah's experience was so deeply personal, we can closely relate to it, seeing how we should pour out both our desires and our heartaches to the Lord, express thankfulness when our prayers are heard, and then act afterwards, sometimes at great sacrifice, thereby worshipping him with our strength as well as with our minds and hearts.

Jesus' Teachings on Prayer in the New Testament

In the aftermath of the national tragedy of the September 11 attacks in 2001, I heard a voice recording of an emergency call that Todd Beamer, one of the passengers on United Airlines Flight 93, placed from an air-phone to an emergency operator after that flight was hijacked. He and several other passengers had decided to rush the cockpit to retake control of the plane, knowing that it would probably result in their deaths. Before they put their plan into action, Beamer asked the operator, Lisa Jefferson, to join him in reciting the Lord's Prayer and the Twenty-Third Psalm.[14]

Hearing the Lord's Prayer being offered in that terrible circumstance was incredibly moving to me. I have always loved this prayer, though it is not one that we repeat or use as a formal part of Latter-day Saint worship. But I realized in that moment that the Lord's model for prayer is something that all Christians share. As I have worshipped with friends of other faiths in their services since then, I have been less inclined than

I used to be to see it as a rote prayer. Rather, I see it as a potentially powerful way for believers to feel closer to God, to the Savior, who taught this as a pattern for our own personal prayers, and to each other.

Jesus himself was a model of prayer, praying regularly throughout his ministry.[15] His example and teachings help us understand how we should prepare for prayer, what kinds of things we should pray for, and how we should follow our prayers by serving God more intently afterwards. For instance, Jesus taught us to prepare ourselves for prayer by directing us to pray in places and in ways that allow us to focus on God rather than seeking the attention of others. Unlike hypocrites (Greek, *hypokritai,* "play actors") who pray to be heard by others, he directed his followers, "When thou prayest, *enter into thy closet,* and when thou hast shut thy door, pray to thy Father which is in secret; and thy Father which seeth in secret shall reward thee openly" (Matthew 6:6; emphasis added). Although the word translated as "closet" (Greek, *tameion*) means either a storeroom or a secret, hidden room,[16] we can also understand this direction in terms of creating personal space for worship when we pray. Whether we are by ourselves at home or in the midst of a crowd in public when we pray, we can prepare by striving to be with just the Lord in that moment, separating ourselves from the world, mentally if not physically, so that we can focus our words and feelings on him alone.

Jesus also taught the importance of true intention in prayer, saying, "But when ye pray, use not vain repetitions, as the heathen do: for they think that they shall be heard for their much speaking" (Matthew 6:7–8). Here the phrase "using vain repetitions" (Greek, *battalogeō*) refers to babbling meaninglessly without sincere intent or purpose behind the words rather than warning us against repeating ourselves.[17] As we know, certain ordinances are always worded the same way, and we all have familiar patterns in our prayers that we often use. For instance, I pray again and again about those people and things that are important to me, such as my family and work, often using the same phrases. In family or group prayers, however, we must realize that we are praying to God rather than being concerned about what those who are hearing us might think.

Though prayer in Old Testament times tended to show love for God through its postures and gestures, Jesus said very little about such outward forms. In the Lord's Prayer (Matthew 6:9–13; parallel Luke 11:2–4), he gave us a simple but beautiful model for prayer:

> *Our Father which art in heaven,*
>
> *Hallowed be thy name.*
> *Thy kingdom come.*
> *Thy will be done in earth, as it is in heaven.*
>
> *Give us this day our daily bread.*
> *And forgive us our debts, as we forgive our debtors.*
> *And lead us not into temptation, but deliver us from evil.*

In this prayer, Jesus taught us to focus on our personal relationship with God by calling upon him as our Father, helping us worship him with our hearts as well as our minds. In 1973, the Quorum of the Twelve Apostles stated, "The title *father* is sacred and eternal. It is significant that of all the titles of respect and honor and admiration that are given to Deity, He has asked us to address Him as Father."[18] We never want to lose the sense of wonder, awe, and majesty that we should feel as we approach God, but understanding that he is our Father bridges that gap between us, reducing the distance and emphasizing the love we feel for each other.

By encouraging us to pray that God's name be kept holy, his kingdom come, and his will be done, the Lord's Prayer helps us understand that prayer is not just about our own needs and concerns. Rather, as we approach the Lord and feel both his power and his love, we are led to worship him with our hearts by submitting to him and aligning our will with his. But it is not enough to pray for God's kingdom to come or his will to be accomplished. Worshipping him with our strength means actively working to build his kingdom here and now by keeping his commandments and following his direction. As always, Jesus was the best example of active obedience to God's will. On the last night of his mortal life, he prayed earnestly that we could become one with him and the Father (John 17:11, 21–23). Then in the face of incredible suffering in the Garden of Gethsemane, after praying that God's will, not his own, be done (Mark 14: 36; parallels Matthew 26:39; Luke 22:41–42), Jesus got up off his knees and went forth to do what would bring about this oneness by carrying our sins and sorrows to the cross and dying for them.

The Lord's Prayer next turns to our own needs, the prayer for our daily bread representing those things we need each day. It calls upon us to seek forgiveness and to forgive others. Finally, it teaches us that it is appropriate to pray that we be spared from trials (Greek, *peirasmon;* KJV, "temptation") and delivered from evil.[19] But Jesus also taught that prayers are answered when we pray in his name (John 14:13–14; 16:23–26), which requires us to consider carefully what we are praying for, making sure that it is in harmony with his will and is the kind of thing that Jesus himself would pray for. Perhaps more importantly, praying in Jesus' name increases our faith that God will hear and answer our prayers because of the love that he has for his Son. Because of Jesus' suffering and death on our behalf, he now stands before the Father as our advocate, pleading our cause before him and, perhaps, praying along with us for those things that we ask in his name (D&C 45:3–5).[20]

Jesus promised that when two or three are gathered in his name, he would be present in their midst and their prayers would be answered (Matthew 18:19–20). An example of the fulfillment of this promise occurred not long after Jesus' ascension, when the eleven apostles gathered in an upper room, where they "continued *with one accord* in prayer and supplication" (Acts 1:14; emphasis added). The expression "with one accord" (Greek, *homothymadon*) means "with one mind or purpose."[21] This expression of unity occurs repeatedly in the book of Acts,[22] where such unified prayer serves as an example of how we should come together in heart and mind as we pray together in our families, at church, and in other groups. As expressed in the sixth verse of Montgomery's hymn "Prayer Is the Soul's Sincere Desire,"

> *The Saints in prayer appear as one*
> *In word and deed and mind,*
> *While with the Father and the Son*
> *Their fellowship they find.*[23]

Being united in prayer requires that we actively participate, even when we are just listening to prayers spoken by others. I have found that when I carefully follow along with a prayer in both my mind and my heart, I feel God's presence in a much more powerful way, and the Spirit changes me much more than if I simply listen passively.

The Example of Jewish, Catholic, Muslim, and Protestant Prayer

Before moving to Jerusalem in 2011, I had attended Catholic, Protestant, and Jewish worship services. But all I knew about Islam was from books, TV reports, and documentaries. We arrived at the BYU–Jerusalem Center in the middle of an August night and had been asleep only a couple of hours when I was awakened by the haunting sound of the *adhān*, or Muslim call to prayer. Five times a day this beautiful Arabic summons rings throughout the city. We subsequently visited several mosques in East Jerusalem, Jordan, and Turkey but never during their actual prayers. From time to time, however, I did catch sight, from a distance, of individuals or groups of Muslims performing *ṣalāt*, or ritual prayer, seeing how Muslims physically showed their love for God and submission to him by bowing down before him.

On Friday afternoons, I liked to sit in a quiet spot on the BYU–Jerusalem Center grounds to read my scriptures, gaze at the Old City, and pray. Frequently during these moments, the *adhān* would ring out, and I knew that at that moment the Temple Mount, which our Muslim friends call Haram al-Sharif, or "the Noble Sanctuary," was filling with worshippers. I knew that they would soon be bowing down before God in the al-Aqsa Mosque and elsewhere on the mount. Throughout that year in the Holy Land, and frequently since, their example has reminded me to stop whatever I am doing during the course of the day to remember the Lord and offer prayers to him in my own way.

PRAYER

Prayer is a natural human impulse, one that brings great spiritual comfort and power to God's children regardless of their religious affiliation or beliefs. As a result, even though proper authority and important truths about God were lost in the centuries after Jesus and his apostles left the earth, prayer remained a central part of Jewish and Christian worship. Similarly, when the new religion of Islam arose, it drew upon Jewish and Christian precedents and likewise emphasized the importance of prayer. After the Middle Ages, the Protestant Reformation further emphasized the importance of personal prayer and changed how people prayed, setting the stage in many ways for the Restoration. Despite our differences with these different traditions, when we see what we have in common with our fellow believers, we can be encouraged in our own prayers and can even learn from the examples of our friends of other faiths and strive to improve our own prayers by praying with more reverence, concentration, and devotion.

After the temple in Jerusalem was destroyed in A.D. 70, prayer became the most important form of Jewish worship. Regular temple services were replaced by communal prayer services that required groups of ten or more Jewish men (Hebrew, *minyān*). According to the rabbis, this occurred because "when ten or more pray together, . . . it says in the Psalms that 'God standeth in the congregation of God' (82:1),"[24] an idea somewhat similar to Jesus' promise that he would be present when two or three are gathered together in his name. In both group and personal prayers, the rabbis sought to increase reverence by composing formal prayers so that even simple, illiterate, or inarticulate men could pray as eloquently as those who were learned.[25] Hebrew also became the preferred language for prayer,[26] much as English-speaking Latter-day Saints today prefer the language of the King James Bible so that prayer can have a more scriptural feel. To compensate for the possibility that set prayers in an unfamiliar language might reduce spirituality, the rabbis renewed emphasis on *kavanah,* or intent, when praying. To prepare themselves and create the correct spiritual space for prayer, worshippers were to avoid distractions, refrain from talk or chatter, shun levity, and, above all, "direct [their hearts] to heaven."[27] These Jewish examples remind me of the importance of showing reverence through the language I use in prayer, pausing for a moment to focus on the Lord, and then concentrating as I pray. This is particularly important with certain familiar prayers, such as blessings on our meals or prayers before and after meetings and classes, which tend to be the same each time.

Among early Christians the Lord's Prayer became more and more important, not just as a model prayer but as a set prayer that was frequently recited.[28] After Christianity became a legal religion, regular group prayer services, known as cathedral prayers, were held each morning and evening in a city's main church.[29] In the monasteries during the Middle Ages, a routine of even more formal prayers developed, which consisted of psalm readings, hymns, and set prayers throughout the day and much of the night.[30] Because this monastic schedule was not one that a lay person could attempt to keep, religious orders were seen as praying on behalf of the rest of the church.

An unintended consequence of these developments, however, was that the average person's role in prayer was reduced to largely passive participation in weekly services, which were held in Latin rather than in local languages.[31] Nevertheless, the reverence that Christians began to show for God by always standing or kneeling as they pray can encourage us to worship with our hearts by being more reverent as we pray. Though we do not follow other Christian practices that developed, such as making the sign of the cross before prayer, understanding that this gesture developed as a way to focus on the Father, the Son, and the Holy Ghost might help us remember that we, too, are praying to our Heavenly Father in the name of his Son and by the power of the Holy Ghost.[32]

Islam began with the revelations of Muḥammad (c. A.D. 570–632) that were dictated and compiled in that faith's scripture, the Qur'ān. Like Judaism and Christianity, Islam, which means "submission," seeks to serve and worship the one true God, known in Arabic as *Allāh* (cognate with the Hebrew *'Ĕlōhîm*).[33] A Muslim is one who submits to God and worships him through five fundamental acts, or pillars, which include a confession of faith, ritual prayer, almsgiving, fasting, and, when possible, pilgrimage. The second of these, ritual prayer, is a translation of the Arabic word *ṣalāt*, which means "bowing, homage, or worship." Performed five times a day, such ritual prayer consists of a set of repeated gestures, actions, and recitations in Arabic. Muslims prepare carefully before *ṣalāt*, performing a ritual washing (Arabic, *wuḍū'*) to cleanse themselves physically and spiritually before approaching God. All of these rituals give depth to their worship by vividly showing their submission to God and their love for him.[34] Ritual prayer is thus a fixed way of worshipping by showing reverence more than being prayerful in our usual sense. To communicate more personally with God, Muslims pray by offering what is known as a *du'ā'*, a "supplication" or "invocation." Such supplications are made by raising the hands together with the palms facing heavenward in a gesture of entreaty, reflecting how we all turn to God in gratitude or need.[35]

To be genuine worship, both *ṣalāt* and *du'ā'* require real intent (Arabic, *niyyah*, the equivalent of Jewish *kavanah*). Some Muslims prepare themselves for prayer by pausing to state to themselves that they are now praying to God. Abū Hāmid Muḥammad Al-Ghazālī (A.D. 1058–1111), an important Persian mystic and theologian, taught that true prayer required inner, mental qualities—such as awareness of God, reverence, awe, understanding, and hope—that turns prayer into worship through the mind as well as through the heart.[36] These practices and insights can encourage us to take our own prayers more seriously by making more of an effort to show reverence for God, reminding ourselves of what we are doing, and cultivating those qualities of mind and heart that foster the presence of the Spirit.

Changes in Christian prayer began with the Protestant Reformation, which started when Martin Luther (A.D. 1483–1546) confronted a Roman Catholic official in 1517 with a list of ninety-five concerns he had about church practice in his time. His reforms were primarily theological and concerned such things as the importance of grace, faith, and the role of scripture, but he and other reformers also began to restructure communal prayer, increasingly using vernacular languages, reducing the number of prayers, and mixing psalms, canticles, and set prayers with more lessons from scripture.[37] Particularly among the Puritans in England and in other reformed churches on the continent of Europe, there was a particular reaction against all set prayers because reformers felt that true prayer should be spontaneous and come from the heart.[38] It is in this context that Montgomery wrote his beloved hymn on prayer, the fourth verse of which represents the role of prayer in the Christian's life:

> *Prayer is the Christian's vital breath,*
> *The Christian's native air,*
> *His watchword at the gates of death;*
> *He enters heav'n with prayer.*[39]

Perhaps most significantly, the Puritan and other Protestant traditions made the home a church and encouraged daily, family prayer.[40] This was the type of home into which Joseph Smith (1805–1844) was born.[41] Thus Protestant prayer patterns set the stage for the Restoration approaches that are familiar and dear to us today.

Prayer in the Restoration

From an early age, our son, Samuel, began to display signs of what was later identified as autism spectrum disorder (ASD). In the spring of 2007, when he was three turning four, his condition began to slowly unfold. While the official diagnosis was still a year off, in March he was assessed by the public school system as having a marked developmental delay and was enrolled in an early intervention preschool. He was soon diagnosed with sensory processing disorder (SPD) and began occupational therapy, soon followed by speech therapy. We were doing all we could, but we were becoming increasingly overwhelmed and heartbroken. Doing all we could, of course, included repeated fasting and prayer. Strength, direction, and occasional small miracles frequently followed, but sometimes the answer to our prayer was simply comfort and, at times, acceptance.

One of those instances occurred on April 5 during my weekly shift in the Provo Utah Temple. Between assignments, I slipped into the celestial room to pour out my heart to the Lord and pray for my son. I was reassured when I felt the Spirit, but I did not receive any particular answer. So, leaving that sacred space, I continued my prayer informally. As I walked alone along one of the third-floor hallways, my prayer became more of a conversation as I felt words and phrases come into my mind in response to each of my silent pleas. When I expressed my sadness that my son might not have all the traditional service opportunities and life experiences that Latter-day Saint parents often expect for their children—such as serving a conventional, full-time mission and marrying in the temple—the answer that came was direct. Many young men and women in the Church do not have those opportunities, the Spirit seemed to say, but often that was because of choices they made. If Samuel did not have those opportunities, it was because he was not able to, and he would not be deprived of any blessing in the eternities. Understanding but still distraught, I cried out in my heart, "But, Lord, he is my only son!"

As chance would have it, that day was Maundy Thursday, the Thursday before Easter that commemorates the Last Supper and Jesus' suffering in Gethsemane. The next day was Good Friday, when the Son of God suffered and died for all of us. The clear response to my cry was firm and struck me to the core: "What about my Only Son?" Answers to my prayers are not always so clear, so dramatic, or so poignant. But over the course of my life, I have tried to develop the habits and patterns of prayer my parents and the Church have taught me. At times the answers that come explain and direct, at times they encourage, and at times they even rebuke and correct. But I am almost always comforted and feel closer to my Father in Heaven as a result of prayer.

Latter-day Saints' understanding of prayer and experience with it have been shaped by the restored gospel of Jesus Christ. The Restoration began with a sincere, personal prayer. In Joseph Smith's 1838 account of the First Vision, canonized as Joseph Smith–History 1:8–20,[42] we learn how the young Joseph's concern over which church he should join led him to act upon the promise of James 1:5 that if any man lacks wisdom, he should ask of God. Feeling that he certainly needed divine guidance, this boy of fourteen retired to a secluded place in the woods one day in the spring of 1820—seeking space, spiritual and mental, as much as finding an actual physical place—to make an attempt. Even though he came from a Bible-reading family that regularly prayed together,[43] Joseph nevertheless recorded, "It was the first time in my life that I had made such an attempt, for amidst all my anxieties, I had never as yet made the attempt to pray vocally" (Joseph Smith–History 1:14). Despite his newness to prayer and in spite of demonic opposition, the young Joseph persevered and received a vision of the Father and the Son, informing him that he should not join any of the existing churches, thus laying the groundwork for the restoration of the gospel of Jesus Christ.[44]

Although the answer to Joseph Smith's question regarding which church to join began the Restoration, we must remember that his prayer was in the first instance a specifically *personal* question about what course Joseph himself should take. We treasure this account not only because of its role in opening our dispensation but also because the First Vision is perhaps the most dramatic example of someone approaching God in prayer, actually experiencing the presence of the Father and the Son, having direct communication with them, and then being sent forth to do their work. Joseph Smith later taught, "It is a great thing to inquire at the hands of God, *or to come into His presence.*"[45] Like the young prophet, we can have our own powerful experiences with prayer if we first prepare ourselves, commune with the Lord as if he were standing before us, and finally finish our prayer with the determination to do what we are directed. In this way prayer serves as the foundation of our worship as it enables us to encounter God and be transformed by the experience.

Like Joseph Smith, we can better prepare for prayer by making space for worship, finding a private, quiet location where we can connect with our Father in Heaven. We can then prepare our minds before prayer by thinking consciously about what we are about to do when we pray, not just what we are about to ask for. Such preparation also includes considering the condition of our lives, which may include needing to mend relationships and repenting (Matthew 5:23–24). Other ways of preparing, if time and circumstances allow, might include reading the scriptures, listening to beautiful music, reading great literature, or simply contemplating God and the beauty of his creation.[46] But even when privacy or other preparation is not possible, we can follow Jesus' instructions to pray in secret by pausing and really remembering to whom we are praying, balancing our awe for God, who is the Creator and master of the universe, with our understanding that he is our Heavenly Father, who loves us.

As he had no doubt been taught by his parents, Joseph Smith knelt down after he entered the Sacred Grove to pray. We likewise usually show our reverence and love for God by bowing our heads and closing our eyes while kneeling in our private and family prayers or by simply sitting or standing still with bowed heads and closed eyes during group prayers. Other ways of praying include clasping our hands, a fairly common Christian sign of reverence and pleading, or folding our arms, which may have arisen from childhood practices meant to help keep children still during prayers. Just as dark powers tried to prevent Joseph from continuing with his first prayer, we too often have difficulty praying, although our opposition usually comes from within ourselves. Once begun, prayer, as with other forms of worship, requires mental and spiritual discipline. Just as the rabbis stressed the importance of concentration as part of *kavanah,* so we must be careful as we pray so that our thoughts do not wander, our hearts are not elsewhere, and our words have not become mechanical.[47] I have found that praying aloud helps keep my mind focused and my language and feelings centered on the Lord in my personal prayers.

Prayer in front of groups, even a group as small as my own family, sometimes presents a different challenge. Too often it is easy to be self-conscious of how I am praying, lapse into familiar, rote patterns, or fall into unnatural, sing-song cadences that I would not use if I were actually standing before the Lord. To help counter this, I find it helpful to pause for a moment to prepare by focusing upon God before I begin. I then try to speak directly to him rather than think so much about the others who are listening.

Another helpful way to foster intentionality during prayer is to stay aware of who it is to whom we are praying, something that we are better able to do because of our restored knowledge of God and our relationship to him. Noting that for centuries good, otherwise sincere

Christians had been struggling to understand the true nature of God, President Gordon B. Hinckley (1910–2008), the fifteenth president of the Church, observed, "And so in 1820, in that incomparable vision, the Father and the Son appeared to the boy Joseph. They spoke to him with words that were audible, and he spoke to Them. They could see. They could speak. They could hear. They were personal. They were of substance. They were not imaginary beings. They were beings tabernacled in flesh. And out of that experience has come our unique and true understanding of the nature of Deity."[48] Indeed, one of the greatest truths the Restoration has given us is that the title "Father" is not just a metaphor—besides being the mighty creator and ruler of the universe, God is, in fact, a loving Parent.

This truly intimate relationship is perhaps best understood by young children as they pray. Elder Marvin J. Ashton (1915–1994), a member of the Twelve, once shared, "I am moved by the prayers of small children. . . . Children seem to have a very personal way of talking to God. They speak to him without fear as a friend. Yes, they seem to speak to him as if he were right there with them."[49] This kind of intentionality—the ability to pray as if in the actual presence of God as Joseph was—is exactly what can make prayer an act of true worship. Still, to maintain respect, Elder Hartman Rector Jr., a member of the Seventy, counseled against the too frequent use of God's name in prayers so that his names and titles do not become repetitious.[50] I also find that if I am not careful, I may rush through the familiar formula of closing in the name of Jesus Christ at the end of my prayers rather than using his name lovingly and reverently.

This balance of reverence for and intimacy with the Lord that we seek can be seen in the language we use in prayer. According to Elder Dallin H. Oaks, a member of the Twelve since 1984, "The Church of Jesus Christ of Latter-day Saints teaches its members to use special language in addressing prayers to our Father in Heaven. . . . The special language of prayer follows different forms in different languages, but the principle is always the same. We should address prayers to our

Heavenly Father in words which speakers of that language associate with love and respect and reverence and closeness."[51] In English, our standard practice, particularly in our public prayers, has been to use language similar to that of the scriptures to create sacred space, differentiating the language of prayer from everyday usage. While King James idiom was not necessarily formal in its origin, over time it came to reflect reverence, and at the time of Joseph Smith, most English-speaking Christians were heavily influenced by the King James Bible and tried to imitate its idiom in their prayers.[52] Because of this, and the fact that similar language is used throughout restoration scripture, English-speaking members of the Church today are encouraged to use some degree of it in their own prayers, at least to the extent of employing otherwise-archaic pronouns such as *thou, thee, thy,* and *thine* when addressing God, forms that have come to signify dignity and respect because they are now commonly used only in scripture.

Our real, intimate relationship with the Lord should lead us to want to be with him often, not only to speak with him in formal prayer but also to enjoy his presence spiritually throughout the day. Restoration scripture, particularly the Book of Mormon, reaffirms the importance of praying frequently while also teaching that being prayerful is as much an attitude or way of living given that one cannot pray continuously, at least not verbally. For example, Jacob wrote, "Behold, my beloved brethren, remember the words of your God; pray unto him continually by day, and give thanks unto his holy name by night" (2 Nephi 9:52; cf. Alma 13:28; 15:17; 62:51; D&C 20:33). Similarly, his brother Nephi taught, "But behold, I say unto you that ye must pray always, and not faint" (2 Nephi 32:9). Amulek, in his discourse on prayer, explained, "Yea, and when you do not cry unto the Lord, *let your hearts be full, drawn out in prayer unto him continually* for your welfare, and also for the welfare of those who are around you" (Alma 34:27; emphasis added). Sometimes informal prayers, offered while involved in another activity such as working or driving, can be the occasions of some of our most needed communication with God. Just being still so we can feel his Spirit is part of being prayerful.

Among the Nephites, the risen Lord commanded, "Pray in your families unto the Father, always in my name, that your wives and your children may be blessed" (3 Nephi 18:21; cf. D&C 23:6; 93:50). As Bruce L. Olsen, former director of Public Affairs for the Church, observed, "Family prayer allows individuals and families to focus attention and affection on God. It builds faith and loyalty within the family and epitomizes Christ-centered family worship."[53] Likewise, group prayer characterizes our services, classes, and various meetings in the Church and also many other activities that we engage in together.

Beyond that, love and concern for our brothers and sisters lead us to pray regularly for the countless people the world over whom we do not know—especially the poor, the sick, the lonely, those suffering from war and terrorism, and those who need the blessings of the gospel. Further, Elder David A. Bednar, a member of the Twelve since 2004, taught of the role of gratitude in prayer, challenging us to periodically try offering only thanks, refraining from asking anything for ourselves, or praying only for other people. Such prayers not only build love for God our Father but they also make us more like Jesus Christ, who is the foremost example of caring for others and serving them.[54]

For prayer to be worship, we must do more than just pray. President Eyring taught, "We must ask with a sincere heart, which means we must have an honest intent to do whatever God's answer requires of us. And our real intent must spring from our faith in Jesus Christ."[55] Inspired by Christ and strengthened by his Atonement, we should be changed by praying and then get off our knees and do the Lord's will. The Latter-day Saint Bible Dictionary clarifies that "prayer is the act by which the will of the Father and the will of the child are brought into correspondence with each other. The object of prayer is not to change the will of God but to secure for ourselves and for others blessings that God is already willing to grant but that are made conditional on our asking for them."[56]

Bringing our will into correspondence with God's obliges us to live as we pray,[57] which requires that we *do* something after prayer. For instance, Amulek concluded his discourse on prayer by teaching, "And now behold, my beloved brethren, I say unto you, do not suppose that this is all; for after ye have done all these things, if ye turn away the needy, and the naked, and visit not the sick and afflicted, and impart of your substance, if ye have, to those who stand in need—I say unto you, if ye do not any of these things, behold, your prayer is vain, and availeth you nothing, and ye are as hypocrites who do deny the faith" (Alma 34:28).

Discerning the Lord's will often requires us to be still after prayer—and sometimes even stop as we pray—so he can direct us. Waiting upon the Lord this way constitutes an important means of being mindful, allowing prayer to better transform us. As we invite the Lord to change our attitudes as we pray, follow the inspiration we receive, and then employ the strength God gives us to follow his direction, we can better follow the example of Jesus in prayer, allowing his grace to change us and make us holy. We then worship with all our strength as well as with our minds and hearts.

Alma pleaded, "Humble yourselves before the Lord, and call on his holy name, and watch and pray continually, that ye may not be tempted above that which ye can bear, and thus be led by the Holy Spirit, becoming humble, meek, submissive, patient, full of love and all long-suffering; having faith on the Lord; *having a hope that ye shall receive eternal life;* having the love of God always in your hearts, *that ye may be lifted up at the last day and enter into his rest*" (Alma 13:28–29; emphasis added). By worshipping regularly through prayer and other important means, such as priesthood ordinances, we will be sanctified and assured of that greater transformation that yet lies ahead.

2

ORDINANCES AND OTHER RITUALS
Sacred Acts and Words That Unite Us with God

And this greater priesthood administereth the gospel and holdeth the key of the mysteries of the kingdom, even the key of the knowledge of God. Therefore, in the ordinances thereof, the power of godliness is manifest. And without the ordinances thereof, and the authority of the priesthood, the power of godliness is not manifest unto men in the flesh.
—Doctrine & Covenants 84:19–21

Though prayer is the most frequent and intimate way that we worship God, ordinances are another way of encountering the Lord and being transformed by him. The word *ordinance* suggests a type of worship that has been ordered and established in a certain way.[1] Such worship consists of specific reverent, symbolic actions—such as baptism or the sacrament—that are accompanied by precise wording. We can pray at any time and in any place, but ordinances are often associated with specific occasions, require proper authority, and sometimes are to be performed only in special places. When administered correctly, ordinances have a powerful transformative capacity: they bring God's grace and power into our lives in this life and prepare us to live eternally in his presence in the next, making us more like him.

Many important ordinances are also closely connected to important events in history—such as the Creation and the Fall, God's deliverance of his people, Jesus' baptism, his Last Supper, or his death on the cross—or look forward to our future resurrection and exaltation. Intentionality is thus important when we participate in ordinances, allowing us to understand better their purpose as we imagine or focus upon the events they represent. Because of their consistency and symbolic nature, such ordinances create a shared memory, linking us with the saving events that they commemorate and with those who participated in them before and after us. Their uniformity and consistency also allow them to play an important role in building a community of faith because they link us with others as we participate in them, transcending differences in culture, language, and time.[2]

Our ordinances have much in common with the rituals of other traditions, despite differences in origin and authority. Seeing these similarities can help us understand our own practices better. The word *ritual* means "ceremony, custom, manner, or style."[3] Generally, rituals are formal ceremonies or symbolic acts that are performed the same way each time.[4] They need not be exclusively religious, however; rituals may be social, political, familial, or personal as well. For instance, attending a patriotic parade or pledging allegiance to a flag may be considered public or social rituals. Families also have traditions that become treasured rituals in our homes. All rituals and many other customs convey symbolic meaning beyond what words alone can express. For instance, shaking hands, nodding our heads, or giving a kiss may convey as much as, or more than, verbal expressions of greeting, agreement, or love.[5] Religious rituals include words, gestures, and even such objects as water, bread, consecrated oil, or sacred clothing, which become holy by how they are used. By preparing ourselves and creating space in our lives for worship, we can increase the spirit we feel as we participate in ordinances.

The third article of faith teaches, "We believe that through the Atonement of Christ, all mankind may be saved by obedience to the laws and ordinances of the Gospel."[6] In other words, ordinances are ways of worshipping God with our minds by teaching us about him, and they also provide ways of actually encountering him and being transformed by him. We are then empowered to go forth to serve him with our strength.

There are several distinguishing features of Latter-day Saint ordinances. First, they must be performed with proper priesthood authority. Second, they have an important connection with covenants: just as an agreement is put into effect by the signing of a contract, so a covenant is entered into and ratified by the performance of an established ordinance.[7] Third, properly performed ordinances bring the saving, healing, strengthening, and exalting power of the Atonement of Jesus Christ into our lives,[8] changing us as we worship him with our hearts, minds, and strength.

Several considerations can help the performance of our ordinances become a more vital part of our regular worship and cause them to bring the Atonement of Jesus Christ more fully into our lives. For instance, how does their symbolism teach us at deeper levels than mere words do? Why is it important that they be performed correctly and with proper authority? How does proper authority and correct performance help us keep the associated covenants more fully? How does preparing for receiving ordinances and participating in them with greater reverence increase their power? What does the importance of rituals in other traditions teach us about how we might be led to appreciate our own ordinances better and perform them with greater reverence and intent? But most of all, how does God transform us, in this life and the next, through the ordinances that he has established, making us more like him?

Principles in Israelite Sacrifice and Ritual

My studies have given me many opportunities over the years to read about worship in the Old Testament. I have always been interested in the sacrifices and worship that the Israelites practiced in the temple. But it is perhaps the Passover story, the story of the Lord's miraculous delivery of the children of Israel from bondage in Egypt, that has always fascinated me the most. And because I am a Christian, it is the parallel between the paschal lamb and Jesus' atoning sacrifice that I have focused on.

ORDINANCES AND OTHER RITUALS

Every semester at the BYU–Jerusalem Center, Ophir Yardin, an Israeli teacher of Jewish history and culture, leads a Passover Seder for the students, the faculty, and their families. I had attended modified seders at Brigham Young University, but they were always led by Latter-day Saints and often focused on gospel connections and symbolism. Ophir's Passover seders were the first ones I attended that were led by an observant Jew. So I set aside my expectations and let myself be taught by him, seeing what this festal commemoration meant to him and his people—deliverance from bondage, God's love for his people, remembering past miracles, and prayers for freedom and justice today.

But throughout the service and dinner that followed, my eyes were repeatedly drawn to the seder plate with its representative items. In particular, I focused on the shank bone, which is placed on the plate to recall the now-discontinued sacrifices of the Jewish temple. Once again I thought of paschal lambs: those of the first Passover, whose blood on the doorframes caused the angel of death to pass by; those whose sacrifice in the centuries that followed reminded the Jews of God's great miracle; and again of the Lamb of God, my Savior, whose blood has saved me from sin and death.

Joseph Smith taught that "the ordinances of the Gospel . . . were laid out before the foundations of the world."[9] Although the early biblical record of the practice and purpose of such sacred rituals is incomplete, Restoration scripture and teachings reveal that the full gospel plan, including its ordinances, was known from Adam to Moses. Likewise, priesthood authority was passed from father to son from Adam until Noah (D&C 107:40–52) and then from Noah to Moses (D&C 84:6–17). It is through this priesthood and its ordinances that we, too, can encounter God, "for without this no man can see the face of God, even the Father, and live" (D&C 84:22).

Nevertheless, according to the Doctrine and Covenants, when Moses tried to institute the higher law in order to prepare the children of Israel to see God, the hardness of their hearts caused the Lord to withdraw the higher priesthood and many of its ordinances. Although some individual families may have enjoyed a greater portion of the gospel plan during this period, the Lord gave a different system, the law of Moses, to the people as a whole and conferred a lesser priesthood upon Aaron and his descendants to administer it (D&C 84:19–27;

124:38). Even though we now enjoy the fulness of the gospel, the ordinances performed under the law of Moses illustrate the great symbolic potential of rituals and teach us much about the importance of covenants, proper preparation, authority, and correct performance when it comes to our own ordinances. Further, Hebrew prophets taught that participating in ordinances alone was not enough; they must be performed with true intent and result in changed, godlier lives.

The children of Israel accepted the law of Moses as part of the covenant they made with the Lord at Sinai (Exodus 24:1–11; 33:1–4), and this covenant was renewed at the end of their wilderness wanderings (Deuteronomy 27–30, which includes a lists of blessings for keeping the covenant and cursings for failing to keep it). As part of the consecration of Aaron and his sons, they were first washed to purify them for their service, dressed in clothing that symbolically represented the priesthood they were receiving, and then anointed to symbolize the pouring of the Lord's Spirit and power upon them (Exodus 29:4–9; 40:12–15).[10] They were thus prepared to represent the Lord to the people by offering sacrifices, teaching God's law, and blessing the people. In a similar manner today, men are called and ordained to priesthood offices as was Aaron (Hebrews 5:4), bearers of the priesthood administer ordinances in the Church to bless its members, and both men and women are endowed and clothed with priesthood power in the temple.[11]

The law of Moses included numerous rituals and careful instructions on how to perform them. The most prominent of these were the sacrifices that were meant to help worshippers draw near to the Lord, something that is suggested by the original Hebrew word for sacrifice (*qorbān*), which means "to come near."[12] Although the five principal kinds of sacrifices described in Leviticus may be unfamiliar to many modern believers,[13] these sacrifices helped teach the nature and consequences of sin, the role of vicarious atonement, and the necessity of repentance to restore us to fellowship with God.[14] Those purposes led the apostle Paul to teach that the law of Moses was a schoolmaster intended to bring us to Christ (Galatians 3:24). Although many sacrifices anticipated the saving death of Jesus Christ, others symbolized the restoration of divine fellowship that his sacrifice has accomplished. For instance, whereas some sacrifices, such as the burnt offering, were completely consumed upon the altar, portions of others were returned to worshippers so that they could share them as a sacrificial meal with their families, which they ate symbolically in the presence of the Lord.[15] Our sacrament maintains this symbolism when we come together to share the Lord's Supper. Not only does this ordinance help us remember his suffering on our behalf but it also symbolizes how we seek communion with him and with each other, each week as we join together to partake of it.

The Hebrew prophets repeatedly warned that performance of any ritual without a real awareness of how it was supposed to bring worshippers closer to God was nothing but an empty form. Sacrifices and other ordinances did not of themselves bring Israelites into divine fellowship unless the ordinances changed their hearts—resulting in lives characterized by obedience, justice, and mercy.[16] This change underscores the importance of both intentionality and mindfulness in worshipping through ordinances. We must not only understand what their purpose is and perform them as if we were actually in God's presence but also strive to be aware of how they are changing us. For instance, we should participate in such ordinances as the sacrament or temple worship with real intent, striving to draw closer to the Lord while being mindful of the presence of his Spirit. When we do so, ordinances can have great power for us, tempering our own selfish desires and making us more righteous, compassionate, and sincere. Above all, ordinances seek to bring us together with God, spiritually in this life and literally in the next.

The Model of New Testament Ordinances

Because it took three attempts for Dad to baptize me correctly, I took extra care when each of my children was baptized. We prepared in multiple family home evenings, reading about baptism, looking at pictures of John the Baptist baptizing Jesus, and practicing how the ordinance would be performed. The joy of lifting each of my children out of the water as a newly baptized member of the Church reduced me to tears, just as my father had wept when he raised me out of the waters of baptism.

Rachel was baptized on a Saturday and confirmed in sacrament meeting the next day. Sometime after that I asked her what she remembered from each of those ordinances, hoping that even at that young age she had experienced something that would serve as an anchor for her faith later in life. The first part of her response was matter-of-fact, almost humorous. What did she remember about her baptism? "The big splash!" was her response. How about her confirmation? She grew solemn and said quietly, "The shock when you said, 'Receive the Holy Ghost.'" Now a woman, my daughter has no doubt had other, perhaps greater, spiritual experiences. But I was grateful then, and am now, that even as a young girl she had felt the Holy Ghost and was baptized with fire as well as water that weekend.

David Seely, a professor of ancient scripture at Brigham Young University, observed that the mortal ministry of Jesus was framed by two essential ordinances: baptism and the sacrament of the Lord's Supper.[17] Because these two ordinances are so closely connected to events in our Savior's life, intentionality is important as we receive them, requiring worship of the mind. As we better understand how they symbolize our own new birth and our need to be fed and sustained by Christ's grace, we are led to treat them with more reverence, making them worship of the heart. Then as we keep the covenants associated with them, we are better prepared to receive his Spirit, which sanctifies us, transforms us, and enables us to serve him with our strength.

Baptism comes from a root meaning "to dip, bathe, or immerse" (Greek, *baptizō*).[18] The first mention of baptism in the New Testament occurs in connection with John the Baptist, who appeared in the wilderness, preaching repentance and baptizing in the Jordan River (Mark 1:2–5; parallels Matthew 3:1–6; Luke 3:2–6). With the cleansing image of being immersed in water, John's baptisms signified forgiveness of sins after repentance, and the symbolism of being washed clean remains an important aspect of baptism today.[19] The baptism of Jesus, however, shows that John's baptism was about more than just the remission of sins: Jesus, who had no sin,[20] submitted to baptism at John's hands "to fulfil all righteousness" (Matthew 3:15). Restoration scripture clarifies how Jesus was baptized to show obedience and fulfill the commandments of God, setting an example for us in the process (also 2 Nephi 31:7–13).

Our understanding of the connection between covenant making and ordinances further helps to explain Jesus' baptism. While Jesus was always obedient to the will of the Father, by being baptized he showed us the necessity of making a covenant of obedience with God. That is an important aspect of baptism for all of us, especially for children, who are baptized into the Church only when they reach the age of accountability. Because they are not accountable for mistakes before that age, their baptism is primarily about covenanting to follow Jesus and keep his commandments from that point on.

When Jesus told Nicodemus that we must be born of water and of the Spirit to see the kingdom of God (John 3:3–7), he taught us that baptism symbolizes that we begin a new, spiritual life after conversion. Paul powerfully expanded upon this symbolism, explaining how being immersed in water and then coming up out of it symbolizes the death and resurrection of Jesus: "Know ye not, that so many of us as were baptized into Jesus Christ were baptized into his death? Therefore we are buried with him by baptism into death: that like as Christ was raised up from the dead by the glory of the Father, even so we also should walk in newness of life" (Romans 6:3–4; see also Colossians 2:12–13; 1 Peter 3:21).

Such symbolism applies to our own baptisms. First, by being baptized, we witness that Jesus died to save us and then rose again. Second, we acknowledge that the old woman or man of sin in us has died and that we are new creatures in Christ, determined to follow him in this life and looking forward to our own resurrection into the next.[21]

In the great commission, given before his ascension, Jesus directed his apostles, "Go ye therefore, and teach all nations, baptizing them in the name of the Father, and of the Son, and of the Holy Ghost" (Matthew 28:19), to which Mark added, "He that believeth and is baptized shall be saved; but he that believeth not shall be damned" (Mark 16:16). As both Jews and Gentiles were brought into Christ's Church,[22] Paul emphasized how the uniformity of baptism—that is, all being baptized the same way for the same end—symbolizes the unity of the body of Christ (1 Corinthians 12:13–14). Indeed, having "put on Christ," we are one in him and hopefully with each other (see Galatians 3:27). In this way the baptismal symbolism of new birth reflects our adoption into the family of Christ. Taking upon ourselves his name and becoming his sons and daughters (Mosiah 5:7), we also become each other's brothers and sisters.[23] The book of Acts illustrates how those who accepted Jesus Christ, confessed faith in his name, and repented were received into his church through baptism,[24] becoming a gospel community characterized by unity, love, mutual support, and worship (Acts 2:43–47; 4:32–37).

Just as Jesus' baptism opened his mortal ministry, so his institution of the sacrament of the Lord's Supper began the final momentous events that brought his ministry to a close. As he finished his last meal with his disciples, Jesus blessed and distributed bread and wine as symbols of the sacrifice he was about to perform (Mark 14:22–25; parallels Matthew 26:26–29; Luke 22:19–20).[25] Of this act Paul wrote: "For I have received of the Lord that which also I delivered unto you, That the Lord Jesus the same night in which he was betrayed took bread: And when he had given thanks, he brake it, and said, Take, eat: this is my body, which is broken for you: *this do in remembrance of me*. After the same manner also he took the cup, when he had supped, saying, This cup is the new testament in my blood: *this do ye, as oft as ye drink it, in remembrance of me*. For as often as ye eat this bread, and drink this cup, *ye do shew the Lord's death till he come*" (1 Corinthians 11:23–26; emphasis added).

As Elder Jeffrey R. Holland of the Council of the Twelve movingly described it, "with a crust of bread, always broken, blessed, and offered first, we remember his bruised body and broken heart, his physical suffering on the cross. . . . With a small cup of water we remember the shedding of Christ's blood and the depth of his spiritual suffering, anguish which began in the Garden of Gethsemane."[26] This pouring out of Jesus' blood established a new covenant (Greek, *kainē diathēkē;* KJV, "new testament") between God and mankind,[27] a covenant we renew every time we partake of the sacrament.

When Paul taught that through this ordinance we "shew the Lord's death till he come," the Greek text means that we "proclaim" (Greek, *katangellō*) it.[28] In other words, by participating in the sacrament, we testify to ourselves and to others that we believe that Jesus truly suffered and died for us. Recalling how Jesus was with his disciples at the first Lord's Supper,[29] we seek similar communion with him each time we partake of it, making the sacrament more than just a commemorative ordinance. In his Bread of Life sermon (John 6:22–71), Jesus taught, "Whoso eateth my flesh, and drinketh my blood, hath eternal life; and I will raise him up at the last day. . . . He that eateth my flesh, and drinketh my blood, dwelleth in me, and I in him. As the living Father hath sent me, and I live by the Father: so he that eateth me, even he shall live by me" (John 6:54–57).[30] By eating and drinking the bread and water of the sacrament, we internalize them and make the Lord part of us here and now. Further, because we will continue to proclaim Jesus' saving death until he returns (1 Corinthians 11:26; Mark 14:25), our ongoing practice of partaking of the sacrament also looks forward to his return and the future messianic banquet that we will share in his kingdom.[31]

In addition to baptism and the celebration of the Lord's Supper, the New Testament describes the laying on of hands, a ritual action used to bestow the Holy Ghost, confer priesthood authority, and bless.[32] In his ministry, Jesus appointed (Greek, *epoiēsen;* KJV, "ordained") the Twelve as apostles, and he further appointed seventy others, giving them authority to preach and do the works that he had done (Mark 3:14–15; 6:7, 12–13; Luke 10:1, 17). Following Jesus' example, his apostles and other authorized disciples later performed healings and worked other miracles by the laying on of hands,[33] which symbolized the physical transferal of God's grace from his authorized servants to others. This transferal of healing grace was also symbolized by the New Testament practice of anointing (Mark 6:13; James 5:14),[34] much as the pouring of oil upon Aaron and his sons or upon Israel's anointed kings represented the conferral of God's power and Spirit upon his servants. In all these cases, those performing the actions did so in place of Jesus Christ, just as priesthood holders act in his behalf today, empowering, healing, or sanctifying us through these ordinances.

Rabbinic, Christian, and Muslim Practices

When I was sixteen and living in Pittsburgh, Pennsylvania, many of my friends were Roman Catholic. On a few occasions when we went out on a Saturday night, my friends' mothers, knowing we would be up late and that their sons might not want to get up early the next morning for church, would say, "Go to Saturday night mass before you go out for the rest of the evening!" Accustomed to going to church and taking the sacrament only on Sundays, I found this injunction a bit surprising. But now I understand that the most important thing to my friends' mothers was their sons' taking communion each week.

Even more surprising to me was the change in the demeanor of my friends that I saw as we entered their church. They were popular and often a little rowdy, but as we entered the church, they reverently crossed themselves with holy water and genuflected toward the altar before sliding into the pew. I was happy to pray and sing along with them during the course of the service, but what happened next surprised me. As my friends went up to take communion, I remained seated, watching with almost embarrassed interest as they approached the railing, knelt, received communion from the priest, crossed themselves again, and returned with hands folded and peaceful expressions on their faces. I had new respect for their faith, and as I went to my own church meetings the next morning and knelt to bless the sacrament, I did it with much greater reverence and appreciation.

Religious rituals of many kinds are important in Judaism, post-apostolic Christianity, and Islam, although among Jews and Muslims the idea of performing the rituals with specific authority is less important than it is for some traditional Christians. Nevertheless, the way people of other faiths perform their religious practices carefully, reverently, and intentionally can teach us how we can administer and participate in the ordinances of our Church with greater intentionality and mindfulness and seek to live the gospel daily with more diligence. By creating space in their lives for worship and making their religion a way of life, our friends of other faiths show reverence to our Father in Heaven and affirm the shared faith and love that we all have for him. In this way we can better worship God through ordinances with our hearts, mind, and strength.

With the destruction of the Jerusalem Temple in A.D. 70, Jews ceased to offer sacrifices as their principal ritual means of drawing closer to God. Much of Jewish worship subsequently occurred in families, making the home an important setting for Jewish worship, much as it is among Latter-day Saints today. For instance, the Talmud, a codification of early rabbinic teachings and commentary on them, taught that offering ritual blessings after meals and at the beginning of Sabbath and holidays made the family table into an altar: "When the Temple stood, sacrifices would secure atonement for an individual; now his table does."[35] The rabbis who succeeded the priests as leaders of the Jewish community further proposed that acts of righteousness and deeds of loving kindness (Hebrew, *ḥesed*) were another way of fulfilling the law,[36] making the way that Jews lived their lives the primary way that they could worship. The rabbis expanded upon Old Testament rules about how food was to be grown, slaughtered, and prepared, and they provided detailed rules governing modesty, personal purity, and marital relations,[37] thereby making almost every act a ritual performance.[38] As with so many of our regular Latter-day Saint practices, all of these observances, when practiced with *kavanah* or proper intent, were meant to help them think of God and how he wanted them to live in all of their daily activities.

While postapostolic Christianity began to greatly elaborate the way baptism, the Lord's Supper, and confirmation were practiced, the solemnity with which Christians observed these rituals reminds us of how reverently we ought to treat the ordinances of our Church. When performed by duly authorized priests and bishops, many Christians saw these rituals as "conduits of grace," or means by which the saving and strengthening power of Christ was brought into the lives of worshippers,[39] an idea similar to our own view of ordinances. Because it was seen as so necessary, baptism was soon administered to infants.[40] Though baptism continued to be done by immersion in Eastern churches, the church in the West maintained the symbolism of washing by pouring or sprinkling in order to make baptism more available to the old, the sick, and the very young. The celebration of the Lord's Supper came to be called the Eucharist, from a Greek word meaning "thanksgiving" (Greek, *eucharistia*) that was also connected to the word for "grace" (Greek, *charis*).[41] Celebrated with the "words of institution" taken from Jesus' words at the Last Supper, the Eucharist became the primary means of communing with the Lord and seeking his grace. In the Roman Catholic tradition, Jesus' words "Take, eat; this is my body" and "This is my blood" (Mark 14:22, 24) came to be taken so literally that the elements of communion were believed to become the actual body and blood of Christ.[42] Another way that Christian churches sought to receive the Lord's grace was through the ritual of confirmation, whereby bishops endeavored to follow the biblical model of the laying on of hands to "strengthen" (Latin, *confirmō*) Christians with the Holy Ghost.[43]

In addition to baptism, the Eucharist, and confirmation, rites of penance, ordination, marriage, and blessing of the sick are considered ordinances in traditional Christian churches.[44] These seven rites are often called mysteries (Greek, *mystēria*) in eastern churches, but in the west, in the Roman Catholic Church, they are generally called sacraments. This term comes from a Latin word meaning a holy act originally used for a soldier's oath of allegiance,[45] making sacraments a way of declaring loyalty to God that also brought God's transforming power into the lives of worshippers. In this sense, traditional Christian

ORDINANCES AND OTHER RITUALS

rites are similar in intent to our ordinances, which bind us to the Lord through covenants even as they help save, strengthen, sanctify, and ultimately exalt us.

Unlike Christianity, Islam did not develop a formal priesthood. The *imām,* or prayer leader, leads prayers, preaches a sermon in the mosque on Fridays and often serves as a community leader, but he does not perform ordinances for others.[46] Instead, individual Muslims engage in a number of ritual practices on their own. As we have discussed, one of the two forms of Islamic prayer, *ṣalāt,* or ritual prayer, is actually a pattern of set postures, actions, and recitations meant to display submission and reverence to God.[47] Another way that Muslims strive to submit to God is by following the example of Muḥammad. The prophet's way of life—including specific words and practices and the way he dealt with friends, family, and society—was set down over time in a body of writing known as the *Sunnah.*[48] Because so much of the Sunnah results in prescribed ways of speaking and acting, it has given Muslims numerous daily rituals meant to make their lives holy through constant acts of submission to God. Nevertheless, Islam's strong emphasis on belief makes the performance of any religious action meaningless without proper intent (Arabic, *niyyah*).[49] That emphasis on intent is something that can be important for us as we strive to live the standards of the gospel, remembering why we are doing what we are doing.

During the Reformation, a renewed emphasis on faith over works led Protestants to new ways of understanding and practicing traditional Christian rites, which they increasingly called ordinances rather than sacraments. Because baptism and the Lord's Supper were the two practices clearly instituted by Christ in the Bible, Martin Luther thought that they were the only necessary ordinances. Nonetheless, he and other Protestant leaders retained both confirmation and some type of ordination by the laying on of hands as practices also found in the New Testament.[50] As the number of Protestant churches multiplied, a variety of views arose regarding baptism and confirmation. Some groups continued to baptize by sprinkling or pouring; others revived the biblical practice of immersion. Although some movements continued infant baptism, others practiced baptism only for those who could understand what it represented and could confess faith. In regard to the Eucharist, which Protestants often call communion, many reformers held that the emblems were merely symbols meant to help worshippers remember Jesus' sacrifice. While Lutherans, Anglicans, and to some extent Methodists retained much of traditional Christian liturgy, other Protestants simplified ritual to keep ordinances more in harmony with what they found in the Bible. Perhaps the biggest change was in regard to authority as many Protestants adopted Martin Luther's idea of "a priesthood of all believers." What was most important for them was faith and the concept of an individual encounter with God.[51] All these changes helped set the stage for the Restoration, but they also show how only revelation could restore ordinances to their original form and power.

The Restoration and Priesthood Ordinances

As the twelfth birthday of my son, Samuel, approached, his autism required that our family do a lot to prepare him to receive the Aaronic Priesthood and be ordained a deacon. We had repeated family home evening lessons about faith, testimony, and the priesthood. We practiced his interview with the bishop, with me sitting across the table from him playing the role of the bishop and asking him all the interview questions. The Monday before the big day, we had one more lesson on priesthood. He was well prepared when I asked him what the priesthood was: "The authority and power to act in the name of Jesus Christ," he replied. I then explained that though we receive authority when we are ordained, we have priesthood power only when we keep our covenants and live righteously.

As with his baptism, there were tears when I ordained my boy a deacon, but there was still work ahead. Four times during the next week I took Samuel to the church, opened the chapel, and got out the trays so that we could practice passing the sacrament. In one of those practice sessions, I tried to explain to him why it was important to be reverent when passing the sacrament. "If Jesus came to our ward one of these Sundays," I said, "He would be at the table breaking the bread and then blessing it and the water, just like he did at the Last Supper. And he might then get up and pass it to each of us, too."

Samuel must have remembered that. Sunday morning I could tell that he was nervous sitting on the bench with the other deacons. When the boys stood up after the first sacrament prayer, the quorum president had to encourage him to walk to the table. But when the tray was in his hand, a change came over Samuel. He stood up straighter and proceeded to pass the sacrament with a reverence I have rarely seen. I wept as my son served me the sacrament of the Lord's Supper. When it was over and he slid into the pew next to me, I put my arm around him and asked how he felt. "I felt proud, Dad," he said. "I felt confident. Most of all, I felt the priesthood."

Because Joseph Smith and most other early Latter-day Saints came from Protestant backgrounds, their expectations for how important ordinances should be performed were similar: they should be based upon biblical practice and be administered with simple dignity. Nevertheless, the Restoration soon made clear that more than being symbolic, ordinances are necessary means of bringing the power of God into the lives of believers. In addition, they require proper authority, are closely connected with vital covenants, and need to be performed according to revealed procedure.

To help understand and appreciate them better, we can consider the restored ordinances of The Church of Jesus Christ of Latter-day Saints according to three general categories. First, ordinances such as baptism and receiving the gift of the Holy Ghost through the laying on of hands play vital roles in overcoming sin and the effects of mortality and are known as *saving ordinances*. Second, ordinances such as priesthood blessings bring additional power and direction from God directly into our lives as needed and can be described as *strengthening ordinances*. Third and finally, certain ceremonies, specifically the sacred ordinances of the house of the Lord, prepare us to become more like our heavenly parents and can be called *exalting ordinances*. Things we can do to experience ordinances more powerfully include working to better understand their symbolism, actively recalling the events that some of them commemorate, understanding that they are performed by priesthood holders acting on behalf of Jesus Christ, and performing them with greater care and reverence.

Authorized baptism for the remission of sins began in this dispensation on May 15, 1829, when the resurrected John the Baptist—who had baptized Jesus Christ—conferred the Aaronic Priesthood upon Joseph Smith and Oliver Cowdery and directed them to baptize each other (D&C 13; Joseph Smith–History 1:73–74).[52] The revealed words "having been commissioned of Jesus Christ" (D&C 20:73) remind us that the one performing the baptism is doing so in the place of the Savior himself. Revelation further clarifies that baptism is properly performed by immersion, underscoring baptism's connection with the death and resurrection of Jesus Christ and symbolizing the new life in the gospel that we begin when we are baptized. Restoration scripture also resolved the debate over infant baptism, teaching that little children were saved by the Atonement of Jesus Christ and emphasizing that proper understanding, faith, and intent should precede the ordinance.[53] Baptism is also the way we enter the kingdom of God, being the way we formally join his Church on earth and the gate by which we enter heaven (2 Nephi 31:17–18).[54]

Perhaps one of the greatest Restoration contributions to the doctrine of baptism is tying it closely to covenants.[55] When we are baptized, we not only promise to take upon ourselves the name of Jesus Christ and keep his commandments but we solemnly resolve to bear one another's burdens, mourn with those that mourn, comfort one another, and stand as witnesses of God in all places and at all times. In return, we are promised eternal life (Mosiah 18:8–9).[56]

With the restoration of the Melchizedek Priesthood by Peter, James, and John (D&C 27:12; 128:20),[57] Joseph and Oliver received the authority necessary to bestow the gift of the Holy Ghost. When the Church was formally reestablished on April 6, 1830, its new members were then confirmed by the laying on of hands and received the gift of the Holy Ghost,[58] which is the right to his constant companionship as long as we are worthy.[59] While the gift of the Holy Ghost includes the privilege of being directed and comforted by the Spirit, as a saving ordinance, receiving confirmation also prepares us for sanctification. The scriptures sometimes describe sanctification as the baptism of fire (Matthew 3:11; 2 Nephi 31:13; 3 Nephi 12:1; D&C 19:31), referring to both its cleansing power and its ability to make us holy. As President Boyd K. Packer explained, baptism and confirmation go hand in hand and should be considered two parts of the same vital process: baptism is the gateway into the Church, but the ordinance of confirmation ratifies our entry into the straight and narrow way, transforms us, and empowers us to press forward in it, eventually leading us back to the presence of the Lord.[60]

Like confirmation, the sacrament was first administered in this dispensation during the first formal meeting of the Church in 1830.[61] Although the revealed sacramental prayers do not contain the traditional "words of institution" that the Catholic Eucharist or Protestant communion takes from Jesus' Last Supper, the first part of the restored ordinance still emphasizes its commemorative role, sanctifying the bread and wine (now water) so that we can partake of them in remembrance of the body and the blood of Christ (Moroni 4–5; D&C 20:75–79).[62] Carefully reflecting upon what Jesus has done for us as we prepare for and then take the sacrament is an important way of creating space in our lives for worship, making this ordinance a true act of communion, first with the Lord as we feel the presence of his Spirit and then with each other as we celebrate the Lord's Supper together as the gathered body of Christ.

Significantly, the second part of the sacramental prayers does something not found in traditional celebrations of the Eucharist or communion: it directly and powerfully connects the sacrament with covenants as it obligates us to take upon ourselves the name of Christ, always remember him, and keep his commandments. In turn, God promises that if we do so, we will always have his Spirit to be with us.[63] In this way, the sacrament is a saving ordinance closely connected with baptism and confirmation. Though the ordinances of baptism and confirmation are generally one-time events in our lives, the sacrament provides a weekly opportunity to renew our baptismal covenants. That opportunity makes our regular Sabbath worship a re-experience of our choice to be baptized. As we then keep these covenants and partake of the sacrament mindfully and with proper intent, the promise of the companionship of the Spirit allows us to realize the injunction given at our confirmation to "receive the Holy Ghost." If taken worthily and sincerely, the sacrament thus opens the door to ongoing sanctification as it brings the Spirit into our lives again and again.

Sister Neill F. Marriott, second counselor in the Young Women General Presidency since 2013, described the sacrament as a weekly opportunity not only to be sanctified but also to receive ongoing guidance and correction, helping us experience true worship as we make our hearts right before the Father and the Son. Sister Marriott taught, "When we open ourselves to the Spirit, we learn God's way and feel His will. During the sacrament, which I call the heart of the Sabbath, I have found that after I pray for forgiveness of sins, it is instructive for me to ask Heavenly Father, 'Father, is there more?'" If we use the time during the sacrament to ask for guidance and yield to the promptings that follow, we then receive gracious strength that allows us to submit to and become more like God.[64] The apostle Paul describes the divine characteristics that then come as the fruits of the Spirit, which include love, joy, peace, longsuffering, gentleness, goodness, faith, meekness, and temperance (Galatians 5:22–23).

Thus the sacrament is not only a saving ordinance but also a strengthening ordinance as it brings the Spirit and its gifts into our lives from week to week and enables us to do God's work, helping us worship him with all our strength. Other strengthening ordinances include the blessing of babies, administering to the sick, giving blessings of counsel and strength, and pronouncing patriarchal blessings. By the laying on of hands, these ordinances give us inspired direction and endowments of divine power that strengthen and transform us in this life and prepare us for the next.[65] The authority to pronounce these

ORDINANCES AND OTHER RITUALS

blessings also comes by the laying on of hands as men have priesthood authority conferred upon them and are ordained to priesthood offices (D&C 20:38–60).[66] Having received the authority and power to act in the name of God, priesthood holders administer the ordinances that bring us to the knowledge of God with the promise that we will enjoy communion with God the Father and his Son Jesus (D&C 88:19–20; 107:18–19).[67] Like some other ordinances, the Melchizedek Priesthood is received with a covenant that "whoso is faithful unto the obtaining these two priesthoods of which I have spoken, and the magnifying their calling, are sanctified by the Spirit" and will receive both the Father and the Son, one day receiving all that they have (D&C 84:33–39).

Becoming like God and Jesus Christ and sharing in all that they have is the very definition of eternal life. The exalting ordinances that prepare us for eternal life were revealed to Joseph Smith between 1836 and 1842. First, in connection with the dedication of the Kirtland Temple in 1836, Joseph Smith instituted early versions of washings and anointings that were reminiscent of the washing, anointing, and clothing of priests at the dedication of the ancient Tabernacle (Exodus 29:4–9; 40:12–15).[68] Then, after a powerful vision of the risen Lord himself, Joseph and Oliver Cowdery received vital priesthood keys and the sealing power on April 3, 1836, under the hands of Moses, Elias, and Elijah.[69] On May 4, 1842, Joseph incorporated a fuller version of washings and anointings into the initiatory ordinances of the endowment ceremony that he administered to a select group of men on the upper floor of his red brick store in Nauvoo. He added to it the clothing of participants in a sacred garment intended to remind them of both the priesthood and the covenants they were making. When his wife Emma received the ceremony on or by September 28, 1843, these ordinances were made available to women as well.[70]

Through these washing, anointing, and clothing ceremonies, both men and women are prepared and clothed with priesthood power in advance of the endowment, which teaches us fundamental truths about the Creation and the Fall, the effects of which are overcome by the

Atonement of Jesus Christ as we make and keep sacred covenants.[71] In the process we more fully take upon ourselves the name of Jesus Christ, covenanting to become like him.[72] As we are mindful and allow these covenants to shape our daily lives and bring us closer and closer to God, they constitute ongoing, vital forms of worship. These exalting ordinances thus represent the culmination of a life of worship, beginning with the saving ordinances of baptism and confirmation and supplemented by regular partaking of the sacrament, priesthood ordinations for men, and blessings for all as needed. Entering the celestial room at the end of the endowment ceremony, we symbolically enter the presence of the Lord, making the endowment a spiritual encounter with God and thus the pinnacle of our worship. When we are sealed as families in the temple, we share in the first ordinance performed by God himself for Adam and Eve in the Garden of Eden. Combined with the endowment and ultimately obtaining the fulness of the priesthood, a temple sealing thus constitutes the exalting ordinance through which the transforming grace of Jesus Christ can sanctify us, guarantee our election, and eventually make us like our eternal parents.[73]

3

HOLY PLACES
Points of Contact between Heaven and Earth

> *One thing have I desired of the Lord,*
> *that will I seek after;*
> *that I may dwell in the house of the Lord all the days of my life,*
> *to behold the beauty of the Lord,*
> *and to inquire in his temple.*
> *—Psalm 27:4*
>
> *Behold, it is my will, that all they who call on my name,*
> *and worship me according to mine everlasting gospel,*
> *should gather together, and stand in holy places.*
> *—Doctrine & Covenants 101:22*

Although prayer and rituals, especially ordinances, may be the most common and important forms of worship, there are other ways of worshipping that provide important settings, occasions, and means for encountering God and being transformed by him. Among these is the use of sacred space not only as an ideal setting for prayer or an appropriate place for ordinances but also as a place to experience God's Spirit with particular power. Such holy places include formal religious structures such as synagogues, churches, mosques, and other meeting houses. They also include natural settings—for instance, mountaintops, wooded groves, views of the sea—that reflect the grandeur of God and are conducive to feeling his presence.[1] Sometimes historical sites that commemorate where God interacted with his people or where they made great sacrifices on his behalf can also become sacred, as can cemeteries, where we remember our dead loved ones and their faith. Indeed, any place where we regularly invite and experience God's Spirit and are stirred to remember what he can do for us can become a holy place. Such holy places, including our homes, remind us of the constant importance of preparing ourselves for worship by creating mental and spiritual space for worship wherever we are.

The Garden of Eden and heaven itself are the two great archetypes of what a holy place should be. As we saw in our discussions of the earliest prayer and ordinances, the Garden of Eden was a place where Adam and Eve walked and talked with God (Genesis 2:16–17, 23–24; 3:8–19; compare Moses 3:16–17, 23–24; 4:14–25). Though our knowledge of the world's early state is incomplete, our understanding is that the garden was a place without death, disease, change, and corruption.[2] It was a point of contact between heaven and earth where God could be with his children. Since the Fall, people in every age and culture have yearned to regain this connection by establishing holy places that recreate the fellowship our first parents once had with the Lord. Whether they be mountaintops, which are literally between heaven and earth, sacred groves, or holy temples that are set apart from the world around them, these sacred spaces seek to recreate our first home. Likewise, men and women have aspired to heaven, looking forward to again meeting God and then dwelling eternally in his presence in the midst of great glory and joy, scenes described vividly in such scriptural passages as Revelation 4 and Doctrine and Covenants 137.

Ancient and modern temples provide the best example of holy places that both recreate Eden and look forward to the celestial kingdom. Our word *temple* comes from the Latin *templum,* which among the Romans referred to a sacred space that was marked out on the earth in reference to the heavens.[3] Noting the connection between *templum* and *template,* Latter-day Saint scholar Hugh Nibley (1910–2005) taught that a temple is a place where the order and pattern of heaven are brought to earth.[4] A temple, then, is the place where we can learn the divine pattern and conform ourselves to it, thus preparing ourselves for heaven. Among the

Greeks, more important than the physical structure of the temple itself (Greek, *naos*) was the precinct (*temenos*) upon which it stood, a spot that was "cut off," or set apart, from its mundane surroundings as the peculiar dwelling place or sanctuary of a king or god. Among the Jews, the Jerusalem Temple was known as the *Bêṯ HaMiqdāš*, "the holy house," because it was held to be the actual dwelling of the Lord.[5]

Our modern Latter-day Saint temples are all of these things, but our other sacred places and those of other believers share the same fundamental features: they are places where we seek to feel God's presence and power with our hearts, learn about his ways with our minds, and go forth empowered to serve with our strength. As we worship in our own holy places—whether they be our temples, chapels, or homes—we should consider what we can do to make them better settings for our prayers and the performance of sacred ordinances. How do they serve as places where we can meet God, coming spiritually into his presence to worship him? How do they help us focus on the Atonement of Jesus Christ and its role in bringing us back to God's presence? In what ways are they points of contact between heaven and earth? What can we do to prepare ourselves to more worthily enter them or spend time in them? What do sacred places teach us about the nature of God and how we can return to his presence?

Sacred Space in Ancient Israel

For several years, my parents served together in the Memphis Tennessee Temple. Two years after Dad died, Mother moved to Provo to be near us. Soon afterwards I invited her to join me on my Thursday shift at the Provo Utah Temple, where I serve as an ordinance worker. After changing from my street clothes, I always stopped at the room where the sisters met before our shift began. I would wave at Mother, and she would always return my greeting with a bright, infectious smile.

A few years later, the effects of Mother's long struggle with cancer and renal failure made it more and more difficult for her to serve in the temple. Because being in the temple was a highlight of her week, the matron and her shift coordinators agreed to let my mother continue, though in her final months she could no longer administer the ordinances she loved. She could, however, sit in a chair and warmly greet temple patrons with that same smile with which she always greeted me. Temple regulars called her an angel, and she rarely revealed how weak she was or how much pain she felt. Rather, she reminded me of the widow Anna from Luke's Christmas story, "which departed not from the temple, but served God with fastings and prayers night and day" (Luke 2:37).

As her strength continued to fail, I often arranged my own assignments so I could give her my arm and walk her from one post to another, frequently taking ten minutes or so to visit with her and join her as she greeted patrons. It was a privilege to sit there in that sacred space together as mother and son. It reminded me of Hannah of the Old Testament, who took her son, Samuel, to the house of the Lord to give him to the Lord (1 Samuel 1:24–28). Thinking back to those precious moments with my mother in the temple, I realize that in a real way she did the same for me.

After the Fall, when mankind was physically separated from the presence of God, prophets built altars where they could come before the Lord for both prayer and sacrifice. These became sacred places, often established in locations where God appeared to his servants, and these spots remained sacred. For instance, Restoration scripture and modern revelation suggest that when Adam and Eve were expelled from the Garden of Eden, Adam built altars for prayer and sacrifice at a place called Adam-ondi-Ahman, which means "Valley of God, where Adam dwelt."[6] Just before his death, Adam gathered his righteous posterity at this sacred place to bless them. The Lord himself appeared to them and ministered to Adam, making this the setting of one of the only known accounts of Adam directly facing God after the Fall (D&C 107:53–56).[7] The Old Testament patriarchs Abraham, Isaac, and Jacob likewise built altars and established holy sites where they worshipped the Lord.[8]

The story of the binding of Isaac (Genesis 22:1–18) provides us with a powerful example of how worship at one of these holy places taught important truths about Jesus Christ and his atoning sacrifice. In this incident, the Lord commanded Abraham to take his beloved son Isaac to Mount Moriah and offer him up as a sacrifice to the Lord. Mount Moriah is associated with the earlier location of Salem, the city of Melchizedek, the king of righteousness who served as a type of

Christ, who is the ultimate king and priest (Hebrews 7). It was also the site of the later Jewish temples. When Abraham showed his willingness to sacrifice everything for God, the Lord himself provided a ram for a sacrifice in Isaac's stead. This experience served as a type of our Father giving his Beloved Son for us, and the worship that Abraham and Isaac offered at that sacred place anticipated how our temple worship focuses on the atoning work of Jesus Christ. In a similar way, the most important thing we do in our ward meetinghouses is partake of the sacrament, thereby weekly commemorating Jesus' sacrifice for us.

Our temples were also foreshadowed by the altars that Abraham and Jacob built at Bethel (Genesis 12:8; 35:1–7), the name of which means "house of God" (Hebrew, *Bêṭ'ēl*). This sacred site provided a vivid instance of how a holy place could be a point of contact between heaven and earth. Here Jacob had a dream of angels ascending and descending a ladder or stairway into heaven, making the sacredness of Bethel a fitting place for the Lord to renew with Jacob the covenants that He had earlier made with Abraham and Isaac (Genesis 28:11–22). In the same way, today we dedicate temples as houses of God where we can make sacred covenants with him and even meet angels in the forms of our departed dead.[9] In our other meetinghouses we regularly invoke the Spirit of the Lord at the beginning of services and classes, asking that he be present as we worship and learn together.

Because the presence of the Lord sanctifies the places where he appears, we should show reverence there as a way of worshipping God. For example, when Moses first encountered the Lord in the burning bush on Mount Sinai, he was instructed to take off his shoes because the ground upon which he stood was holy (Exodus 3:1–6). Likewise, when we enter our temples, we set aside the world, both literally and figuratively. Changing from our street clothes into white clothing and exchanging our shoes for slippers, we leave behind the fallen world and its honors as we reverence the Lord and his house. In our chapels and other meetinghouses, we should behave differently than we would elsewhere, speaking more softly and behaving more reverently. Because we also strive to have the Spirit in our homes, which alone "compare with the temple in sacredness,"[10] we must be careful what kinds of media, music, and other worldly influences we bring into them.

With its peak stretching up to heaven, Mount Sinai was a meeting place of heaven and earth. That may have led Isaiah to call the temple in his day "the mountain of the Lord's house," where all people were invited to worship the Lord and learn of his ways (Isaiah 2:2–4; 56:7; 66:20).[11] One way we learn about the ways of the Lord is from the layouts of temples themselves. For instance, the floor plans of the Tabernacle that Moses built in the wilderness and the temples that were later built in Jerusalem symbolized the increasing levels of holiness that were needed to approach the Lord. Worshippers first entered an outer court, where the people as a whole prayed and where priests purified themselves before they made sacrifices or entered the main sanctuary of the temple (Exodus 30:19–21; 40:31). The priests alone proceeded into the Holy Place, where they performed certain rituals.[12] Once a year only the high priest passed through a veil into the Holy of Holies, which represented the actual presence of God.[13] He did that with the blood of the Day of Atonement sacrifice, prefiguring how we, too, come into God's presence only by virtue of the atoning blood of Jesus Christ (Hebrews 9:1–14).

In this way, Old Testament temples demonstrated how we draw closer to the Lord through prayer, ordinances, and the power of the priesthood. All prayer requires that we create sacred space, whether physical or spiritual, and we all need baptism and repentance, which were anciently represented by the priests' washing and sacrificing before approaching God further. The Holy Place of ancient temples, decorated with palm trees, flowers, and cherubim (1 Kings 6:29–30), was a microcosm of the Garden of Eden and a template of how this lost condition could be regained through rituals and advancing through progressive levels of holiness, much as Latter-day Saints do through the endowment today. Finally, the Holy of Holies, like the celestial room in modern temples, points us forward to our hoped-for heavenly state in the presence of God.[14]

New Testament Places of Worship

While I was an undergraduate at Brigham Young University, I had the opportunity to spend six months in a study abroad program in Baden, Austria. Just down the street from the center where we lived and had our classes was a beautiful old Roman Catholic Church. On occasion as I passed it returning from the train station or an errand, I would slip inside and enjoy its quiet stillness. There was a feeling of holiness in it that I knew came from more than a century's worth of faithful people worshipping there.

During that semester abroad, my fellow students and I had the opportunity to travel widely in Europe, where I saw many great cathedrals and small churches, some far older than the little parish church in Baden. That made me think of the places where I have worshipped throughout my life, ranging from a rented college auditorium in Pennsylvania to standard Latter-day Saint meetinghouses in Utah to rented houses in Thailand, where I served my mission. Those makeshift Thai branch chapels reminded me of what I read about in the book of Acts, where the earliest congregations of Christians met in each other's homes, and I realized that it was not the building that made a place of worship sacred but rather what took place there. Wherever two or three are gathered in Jesus' name to pray, sing, and receive ordinances, those are the places that worship makes holy.

As observant Jews, Jesus and his disciples frequented the same places of worship as other Jews. The Gospels record that they were often found in synagogues on the Sabbath. Although the exact development of these meeting places is unclear and the archaeological evidence for them in Galilee at the time of Jesus is incomplete, synagogues had become particularly important for communities of Jews who lived too far away from the temple to frequently go there to worship.[15] Jesus not only respected the traditional acts of worship in a synagogue but was an active participant, as is clear from his visit to the synagogue in his hometown, where he first stood to read from Isaiah and then sat down to explain the passage (Luke 4:16–27). Despite the distance—some ninety miles between Galilee and Jerusalem—Jesus also regularly attended the festivals held at the temple in Jerusalem, going first with his family as a child (Luke 2:41–50) and later with his disciples during his ministry (John 2:13; 5:1; 7:14; 10:22–23). He was critical of corruption and religious abuses there, but he recognized the temple as a house of prayer (Mark 11:17; parallels Matthew 21:13; Luke 19:46) and acknowledged it as his Father's house (Matthew 23:21).[16] Nevertheless, at his trial he also spoke of a temple built without hands (Mark 14:58), and earlier in his ministry he had taught the Samaritan woman that more important than *where* we worship is *how* we worship—that is, in spirit and in truth (John 4:20–24).

After Jesus' resurrection and ascension, the early Christian community in Jerusalem continued to worship in the temple, using it as a place for prayer (Luke 24:53; Acts 2:46–47; 3:1; 22:17), although it is unclear how much they used it for other ritual purposes.[17] But regular prayer, the "breaking of bread" (which could refer to fellowshipping meals as well as the sacrament), and praising God took place in private houses as well (Acts 2:42–47). Indeed, as Christianity began to spread, the house church came to be the most prevalent place of worship. There worship services would have included prayer, partaking of the Lord's Supper (sometimes as part of a larger fellowship meal), sharing testimony, teaching, and singing hymns.[18] As with the Jewish synagogue, any sanctity felt in the house church was largely a function of its serving as the setting for worship and basic ordinances. Such is the case today with our varying types of meetinghouses—ranging from the fine craftsmanship of pioneer-era tabernacles in Utah to rented space in mission fields to often utilitarian ward meetinghouses throughout the world.

Although the New Testament gives us few details regarding the actual places where early Christians worshipped, its authors sometimes used the language of holy places in reference to the gathered church. Notably, Paul used such language to describe the Saints as different members of the spiritual body of Christ (1 Corinthians 12:12–27), giving Paul's mention of "temples" a meaning different from what we sometimes have when reading his writings. For instance, he wrote to the Corinthian Saints, "Know ye not that *ye are the temple of God,* and that the Spirit of God dwelleth in you? If any man defile the temple of God, him shall God destroy; *for the temple of God is holy, which temple ye are*" (1 Corinthians 3:16–17; emphasis added; see also 1 Corinthians 6:19). Because Book of Mormon authors often teach the important principle that our individual bodies are temples of both our own spirit and of the Holy Ghost (Mosiah 2:37; Alma 7:21; 34:36; Helaman 4:24), we naturally see this same idea in Paul's references to temples. In Paul's writings, however, he speaks of the Corinthian Saints in the plural as collectively being God's temple in the singular, and his concern is about how individuals can deprive the group of God's Spirit.[19]

This reading of Paul's admonition has important implications for creating and maintaining sacred space for worship. As members of the body of Christ, whenever we meet together to worship—regardless of where we might actually be meeting physically—we should do so after we have made an effort to set aside sin and unite in peace and love to seek the Lord. As Jesus taught, "Therefore if thou bring thy gift to the altar, and there rememberest that thy brother hath ought against thee; leave there thy gift before the altar, and go thy way; first be reconciled to thy brother, and then come and offer thy gift" (Matthew 5:23–24). Otherwise we keep the body of Christ from being a holy place where God's Spirit can be and where true worship can take place. Because we are one body, each individual's sin, unkindness, and selfishness hurts the whole, even as our faith and love and compassion edifies it. When we are unified, it does not matter whether two or three believers gather, or two or three hundred. Nor does it matter whether we worship in a stately cathedral, an Amish threshing floor, a theater-like megachurch, or a Latter-day Saint ward building.[20] As we purify the space in our heart by reaching out to our sisters and brothers as well as to God, not only will we have a better chance of encountering God but we will also be filled with love, understanding, and compassion for one another.

Sanctuaries through the Ages

Having lived in different parts of the United States as I was growing up, I was familiar with different churches and synagogues. But those experiences and even years of study did not prepare me for the religious diversity that I encountered when my family and I lived in Jerusalem for a year. The Old City is the site of the Western Wall, the Church of the Holy Sepulchre, and the Al Aqsa Mosque, some of the holiest sites of the Jewish, Christian, and Muslim faiths. Within this walled area of only 0.35 square miles are places of worship seemingly around every corner representing every variety of those religions. Beyond the walls of Jerusalem and extending throughout the Holy Land are numerous shrines, tombs, and commemorative monuments that remind believers of important events in their traditions.

I felt the Spirit in many of these sanctuaries, even when I did not share the beliefs or practices of those who worshipped there. I have come to believe that the faith of those who pray and seek God in a place can make that place holy. This belief has encouraged me to help add in some small measure to the holiness of the places I hold sacred in my faith. Whether it is my ward chapel, the temple where I serve, my home where I live, or my favorite thinking and praying spots along the trail where I often go running, these sacred spots can be places where I find God and commune with him.

From the time of the apostles until the Prophet Joseph Smith, believers in the three main monotheistic religious traditions built and worshipped in a variety of different kinds of sanctuaries. Whether synagogues, small churches, great cathedrals, or mosques, establishing holy places was an important way of honoring God and creating space for prayer, ordinances, and study. Often we can learn from our fellow believers how we can show more reverence in our own meetinghouses, churches, temples, and homes. As we do so, we can better feel the Lord's Spirit, learn his ways, and prepare to serve him, thereby helping us worship him with our hearts, minds, and strength.

When the Jerusalem Temple was destroyed in A.D. 70, Judaism lost its most holy sanctuary, the place where the presence of God was believed to reside. Its ruins remained a place of mourning, but over the centuries one surviving retaining wall of the temple platform, known as the Western Wall, or *Kotel,* has become the site not only of regular prayer but of festal assemblies, bar mitzvah celebrations, and other religious activities.[21] This lingering remnant of the temple notwithstanding, since A.D. 70 the most common holy places for Jews have been the synagogue and the home. As the focus of community religious life, the synagogue is a place where Jews gather for communal prayer and scripture reading.[22] But reading sacred texts and, increasingly, the words of the sages is not limited to formal worship services. In fact, in the Ashkenazi tradition of eastern Europe, a synagogue is often known in Yiddish as a *Shul*—a school.

The home also became a particular focus of Jewish devotion in the period after the temple. Although not new, such ritual acts as marking a Jewish home with a *mezuzah* on its door frame (making it the setting of regular prayer), keeping kosher within it, and keeping all the rules of personal and family purity contributed to the sanctity of the home, setting it apart from the rest of the world.[23] Today we as Latter-day Saints likewise strive to make our homes sacred islands of refuge by making them the scenes of family and personal prayer, family home evening, Christ-centered holidays, and by keeping negative influences of the world outside them.

To provide space for large gatherings of worshippers and an appropriate setting for administering the sacraments, Christians adopted the architectural plan of the Roman basilica that had originally served Roman law courts.[24] Its open, rectangular floorplan allowed for large gatherings in the hall. In Christian basilicas, the worshippers' attention was focused on the altar in the apse at one end of the hall, or nave, thus emphasizing the celebration of the Eucharist and other sacraments. A lectern for reading from the scriptures and a pulpit for preaching lessons drawn from the readings flanked the altar, illustrating how worshippers also gathered to be fed by the word of God.[25] Over time the basilica plan in western Europe developed into the familiar cruciform, or cross-shaped, plan of medieval and Gothic cathedrals. This symbolic floor plan was matched in both the east and the west by the development of religious art in the form of mosaics, paintings, statues, and stained glass windows. Such religious art was meant to honor God, inspire worshippers, and, in a period when literacy was rare, teach biblical stories to those who could not read them.[26]

While most Christian churches were made holy by the worship that occurred in them, some were built to commemorate important sacred events that had taken place at those sites. This was particularly the case in the Holy Land, where the Basilica of the Nativity in Bethlehem and the Church of the Holy Sepulchre in Jerusalem commemorated Jesus' birth, death, and resurrection. Other churches at the sites of miracles or the graves of saints became common throughout Palestine,[27] emphasizing the role of memory in worship. This aspect of worship gave rise to the impulse for pilgrimage as Christians made sometimes incredible efforts to visit sites in the Holy Land, believing that if they could get close to places made sacred in history they could get closer to God. Recalling what God has done in the past builds faith that he will similarly act in the present. We do something similar with such important sites as the Sacred Grove and other places in Church history, where markers and often visitors centers have been built to accommodate visitors.

This high regard for sacred space, memory, and pilgrimage is similarly evident in Islam, where Muḥammad made the traditional shrine called the Ka'ba in Mecca the most holy place in the Muslim faith.[28] According to one tradition, the Ka'ba was the site of a temple built by Adam and Eve, which was later rebuilt by Abraham.[29] One of the Five Pillars of Islam requires every Muslim who has the means to make a pilgrimage, or *Ḥaǧǧ*, to Mecca to worship at the Ka'ba and other sites in and near Mecca. Through this use of sacred space, Islam seeks to bring worshippers closer to God and transform them into better Muslims even as it unites believers from different races, languages, social classes, and sexes.[30] The importance of the Ka'ba is so great that every other place of Muslim worship, or mosque (Arabic, *masjid*), is oriented towards it. The Arabic word means "the place of bowing down in prayer" and indicates its primary use as the setting for *ṣalāt*, worship through ritual prayer.[31] The mosque is also the place where the prayer leader, or *imām,* delivers a sermon after Friday prayers. Careful rules of dress, behavior, and etiquette inside a mosque ensure that worshippers reverence God and can maintain concentration during prayer, just as we wear "Sunday best" clothes and act reverently in our churches.

The Protestant Reformation brought changes to Christian conceptions of sacred space, resulting in changes in church architecture. Initially Protestants simply adapted Catholic cathedrals and parish churches to their own sensibilities, which in extreme cases meant removing crucifixes and statues of saints, destroying stained glass, and whitewashing over paintings so that nothing remained that seemed idolatrous or might distract from the preached word.[32] Generally, Protestant meeting places focused on the pulpit to emphasize the preaching of the word of God, relegating the communion table to a position under the pulpit or in some less central position.[33] Indeed, for many Protestants, sacred space was less important than prayer, preaching, and praise through music, which could be done anywhere. This attitude was particularly the case in early America, especially in such newly settled areas as upstate New York, where members of the Smith family attended services in open air camp meetings as often as in the few established churches.[34] As the Restoration unfolded, however, Joseph Smith's understanding of the importance of holy places deepened.

Holy Places in the Restoration

As do many Latter-day Saint parents, my wife, Elaine, and I have taught our children about the holiness of the house of the Lord through the words of Janice Kapp Perry's lovely children's song "I Love to See the Temple":

> I love to see the temple.
> I'm going there someday
> To feel the Holy Spirit,
> To listen and to pray.
> For the temple is a house of God,
> A place of love and beauty.
> I'll prepare myself while I am young;
> This is my sacred duty.

I love to see the temple.
I'll go inside someday.
I'll cov'nant with my Father;
I'll promise to obey.
For the temple is a holy place
Where we are sealed together.
As a child of God, I've learned this truth:
A fam'ly is forever.[35]

This song was not in the children's songbook when I was growing up, but I learned these important truths from my parents and teachers. Then when I was a youth, I had opportunities to go to the Washington D.C. Temple and the Atlanta Georgia Temple to perform baptisms for the dead. Then came one of the momentous days of my life. On the day after Thanksgiving, November 23, 1984, I entered the St. George Utah Temple to be endowed. My parents, living out of state, could not be there, but many family members, who had gathered at my maternal grandmother's for Thanksgiving, shared the event with me. My paternal grandparents were ordinance workers in that temple, so my grandmother greeted me as I entered, and my grandfather performed my initiatory ordinances and officiated in my endowment session.

Much of what I experienced that day was new to me, but the feelings I had were what I had hoped for—and more. The Spirit in the temple that day was palpable to me, like a warm, enfolding blanket. I still feel that strong spirit in the temple whenever I take the time and make the effort to feel it. What I did not expect that first day, however, was that I would carry some of that special spirit out of the temple with me in the form of a holy garment, a sacred reminder of the covenants that I had made that day and the priesthood power with which I had been clothed. I have learned since how it also serves as an outward symbol of the atoning blood of Jesus Christ that not only covers my sins but will sanctify me if I am faithful, holding out the promise of eternal life in God's presence.

Latter-day Saints initially met wherever convenient for their worship services. The organization of the Church, for instance, took place in the log home of Peter Whitmer, Senior, in Fayette, New York.[36] Homes, schoolhouses, groves, boweries, and the public assembly rooms of the Kirtland and Nauvoo Temples were used for sacrament meetings and conferences. Indeed, before 1847, few meetinghouses were used for weekly Sunday worship. By and large, and in accordance with their Protestant backgrounds, early Latter-day Saints seem to have emphasized *what* was done—particularly preaching, praying, administering the sacrament, and singing—over *where* this worship took place. After the Saints arrived in the Great Basin, they began to construct simple, one-room meetinghouses that on the frontier served as churches, community centers, and schools.

As the areas settled by the Saints became more developed, they constructed more substantial, often well-crafted buildings for ward and stake use, including pioneer-era tabernacles and the Assembly Hall and Tabernacle on Temple Square. Over time, styles continued to change, and a growing emphasis on efficiencies of use and cost led to the creation of standard meetinghouse plans.[37] Despite these changes, "a Latter-day Saint meetinghouse still serves the same function as the New England meetinghouse—as a multipurpose center for worship and cultural activities."[38] This emphasis on functionality and a relative lack of traditional religious aesthetics can, if we are not mindful, reduce the potential of our meetinghouses for seeming like sacred space. Nevertheless, the gradation implicit in calling the larger room in which we hold sacrament meeting the chapel and other rooms the cultural hall, classrooms, and offices can help us differentiate how we should act and worship in those respective spaces. As a dedicated place, the entire meetinghouse should be treated with respect, but certainly the degree of reverence displayed in the chapel where we partake of the sacrament and hold worship services can and should be greater than in other areas of the meetinghouse. The purpose of worship can be accomplished by focusing on *what* we do in the chapel, to be sure, but *how* we act, dress, talk, and feel in that space—not just during meetings but at other times as well—can add to its holiness and thereby add to our experience.

President Boyd K. Packer taught: "For Sunday meetings, the music, dress, and conduct should be appropriate for worship. Foyers are built into our chapels to allow for the greeting and chatter that are typical of people who love one another. However, when we step into the chapel, we *must!*—each of us *must*—watch ourselves lest we be guilty of intruding when someone is struggling to feel delicate spiritual communications."[39] Especially when we enter the chapel for a sacrament service, we can create space for worship there by leaving the world behind, turning off our cell phones, avoiding unnecessary conversation, and avoiding other distractions as we concentrate on the Lord and seek his Spirit.

Joseph Smith's inspired revision of the Bible influenced his understanding of sacred space and served as a catalyst for revelations that dramatically changed the way we experience sacred space in our most holy setting—the temple. No doubt references in the Old Testament to the Tabernacle and subsequent temples led Joseph to think about their importance, and in late 1832 and early 1833 he received a revelation directing him to build "a house, even a house of prayer, a house of fasting, a house of faith, a house of learning, a house of glory, a house of order, a house of God" (D&C 88:119; see also 95:3, 8–17). In extremely difficult circumstances, the early Saints sacrificed to build and beautify this temple in Kirtland, Ohio, desiring to make it an acceptable offering to the Lord and a place where he could meet his people. The Kirtland Temple and later the Nauvoo Temple were not built with the specific ceremonies of exalting ordinances in mind; they were initially conceived of as particularly fitting settings for worship and instruction, places where the Saints could gather out of the world and spiritually come before God, learn, and partake of his Spirit in greater measure than they could elsewhere.

The Latter-day Saint temple, however, began to reflect its full divine intent when the performance of ordinances related to the endowment, sealings, and fulness of the priesthood instituted by Joseph in his red brick store in Nauvoo were relocated to the attic floors of the temple even before its completion.[40] These important ordinances came to be the focus of subsequent temples because of the very nature of temples: as sacred spaces set apart from temporal space and time, they are the appropriate settings for ordinances with eternal implications. As "mountains of the Lord's house" (D&C 133:13), they are places where we leave behind time and the world as we ascend towards God, who reaches down from eternity and heaven to make covenants with us and bless us. Further, in the process of participating in the dramatized presentation of the endowment, we come to see existence in an eternal context. Like Adam and Eve, we began in the presence of our heavenly parents but needed to leave them to progress. In this world we strive through the making and keeping of sacred covenants to avail ourselves more fully of the Atonement and grace of Jesus Christ, not only to save us but also to exalt us. And with the knowledge and power we gain in that holy setting, we are prepared to return to God's presence as immortal, glorified heirs of his kingdom.[41]

The temple, however, is more than just the symbolic top of a mountain where heaven and earth meet. It is also a place where the spirit world, which Brigham Young taught is in another dimension here on this earth,[42] reaches across the veil and meets both us and heaven, making possible vicarious work for the dead. After a vision of his deceased brother Alvin in heaven (D&C 137), Joseph Smith had begun to think about how the dead could be saved, particularly when they had not had the chance to receive vital saving ordinances. He shared his revealed answer to this question in a sermon in Nauvoo on August 15, 1840, in which he explained that living Church members could receive such ordinances for their deceased family members. Accordingly, baptisms for the dead began to be performed in the Mississippi River in September 1840, but Joseph later explained that the appropriate place for such vicarious work was the temple. As soon as a preliminary font could be prepared in the basement of the Nauvoo Temple, still under construction, the performance of vicarious baptisms was transferred there in January 1841.[43] Exalting ordinances for the dead began to be performed in January 1877 in the St. George Temple.[44]

The doctrine of preaching the gospel to the dead and the vicarious performance of ordinances on their behalf, effective only if they choose to accept them, is one of the most stunning and beautiful contributions of the Restoration. In his vision of the Savior's own work among the dead, Joseph F. Smith (1838–1918), sixth president of the Church, related that during the time between his crucifixion and resurrection, Jesus Christ declared liberty to the captives who had been faithful and prepared a way for all other departed spirits to hear the gospel (D&C 138:11–37). Of our part in this work, Andrew Skinner, a professor of ancient scripture at Brigham Young University, wrote, "When we enter the temple and speak the names of the deceased as though they themselves were making the covenants of eternity, we make it possible for them to be set free."[45]

Besides opening the way for the salvation of the dead, worship through vicarious work for the dead blesses us in two important ways. First, our own ordinances are one-time rites of initiation. The opportunity to return to the temple again and again to vicariously perform the same ordinances for others gives us a chance to review what we first learned, receive new inspiration, and recommit ourselves to the covenants we made. In this regard, we are particularly blessed to live in a time when temples are generally more available in most parts of the world than they were in earlier decades. Much as some faithful Muslims save their entire lives to make a single pilgrimage to Mecca, faithful Latter-day Saints often make great sacrifices to go the temple at least one time in their life. Second, performing proxy work produces a real transformation in us, making us literal "saviours . . . on Mount Zion" (Obadiah 1:21) as we, in a small way, become like Jesus Christ, who through his atoning sacrifice vicariously did for us what we cannot do for ourselves.

But temples, as real meeting places between heaven and earth, are more than just eternal settings for ordinances and ideal places for powerful prayer, having obtained the keys by which we "may ask and receive" (D&C 124:97). Whether we go to the temple to receive our own ordinances, to perform vicarious ordinances for the dead, or to serve as ordinance workers or in some other capacity, we can and should make time to worship and not just "do temple work." Ideally we should make the temple a potent place of prayer, meditation, contemplation, and communion, which requires that we see it as more than just a special building. To accomplish that requires preparation: just as the Jewish priests washed their hands and feet before entering the temple and then performed its rituals with *kavanah,* so should we prepare by purifying ourselves and turning our thoughts and concentration to the Lord. Once there, temple worship requires that we know its purpose and also conceive of it as a place outside of this world where God and his Spirit actually reside.

That is the root sense of intentionality, and if we are mindful of the special spirit that is present in that holy place, it can be, as Andrew Skinner terms it, "a place of personal revelation and education" and "a portal to heaven."[46] I have found that my temple experience is indeed worship if it transforms me—whether it be a sense of sanctification, renewed purpose, deepened commitment, or a changed heart and spirit. Then we leave the temple carrying that transformation with us in the form of the temple garment we wear. Some years ago when my frantic work and personal schedule made me question whether I could continue to serve weekly in the temple, I discussed with my wife, Elaine, the possibility of taking a leave of absence. I recall her saying something to the effect, "We cannot afford for you to do that. You are a different, better person when you return home from the temple than when you left."

Coming *home* from the temple a transformed person is indeed a wonderful result of temple worship, because as Latter-day Saints we believe that "only the home can compare with the temple in sacredness."[47] Like our Jewish friends, much of our worship takes place at home. Ideally our homes are dedicated "as sacred edifices where the Holy Spirit can reside, and as sanctuaries where family members can worship, find safety from the world, grow spiritually, and prepare for eternal family relationships."[48] The potential for the Spirit's presence must be realized, requiring intent, mindfulness, and a minimum degree of worthiness on our part. But when we attain those qualifications, the home becomes an ideal scene for worshipful activities, including daily personal and family prayer, as well as strengthening ordinances, such as administering to the sick, father's blessings, and blessings of comfort and counsel. In addition, in cases of disability or extended illness, the sacrament may be brought into the home. As we will see, it is also an ideal setting for studying and teaching the scriptures, keeping the Sabbath and celebrating Christ-centered holidays, praising the Lord and inviting the Spirit through music, and serving one another.

As a domestic temple, the home is a vital point of contact between heaven and earth where we can strive to encounter God and be transformed by him. Because of the bonds of love built among family members and other loved ones, I have found that the home can also be a place where this world and the spirit world meet. My mother, after years of illness, moved into my home to live with my family in 2013. A little over a year later, it became apparent one morning that she was failing and that the end was near. She asked for a final blessing, and during that tender experience I shared the Lord's approval of her life of faithfulness and sealed her blessings upon her. I assured her that her passing would be easy and that loved ones were near. A few hours later I returned from an errand to find her unresponsive. I called hospice, and while the kind nurse tended to her, Mom passed away with me standing beside her and my daughter, Rachel, holding her hand. While the grief and sadness I felt at that moment were almost overwhelming, they were immediately tempered by a powerful wave of the Spirit and the sense that she was moving easily into the loving arms of her husband and parents who had predeceased her. It was a beautiful moment that I will always remember, and in that moment our home was truly a holy place.

4

SACRED TIME
Remembering, Recreating, and Anticipating Meetings with God

Offer up thy sacraments upon my holy day; for verily this is a day appointed unto you to rest from your labors, and to pay thy devotions unto the Most High; nevertheless thy vows shall be offered up in righteousness on all days and at all times.
—*Doctrine & Covenants* 59:9–11

Just as holy places provide important settings for worship, so sacred time affords occasions conducive to drawing us closer to God. Although we are to be witnesses of God "at all times and in all things, and in all places" (Mosiah 18:9) and hence should worship him anytime, in any circumstances, and anywhere, the role of memory, recognition, and anticipation in worship makes the concept of sacred time important. In the same way that holy places are set apart from the rest of the world, a certain important moment (Greek, *kairos*) can be separated from the flow of time (Greek, *chronos*) to recall what God has done for us in the past, to appreciate what he is doing now, and to look forward to what he has promised to do in the future.[1] The regular rhythm of days, weeks, months, and years that is apparent in the cycles of the sun, the moon, and the seasons has long structured biological life. Similarly, the Sabbath, holidays, and rites of passage provide structure and give meaning to our worship and spiritual life. As with holy places, sacred times remind us that every act of worship should be different from our usual activities, requiring preparation to create the mental and spiritual space for us to feel God's Spirit.

Often we use such terms as *mark* and *keep* in connection with sacred time, describing how we identify what times are different from the ordinary, and we choose to make those times sacred. Deliberately marking and keeping sacred time helps us know God better and more deeply, allowing his Spirit to sanctify and change us. Sacred time includes our weekly Sabbath, when we take time to pray, read, and attend worship services to take the sacrament and study the gospel together. It certainly embraces the magic of Christmas Eve and Christmas morning; the solemnness of the Thursday and Good Friday before Easter; and the joy of the resurrection Easter morning. But it also includes those regular moments found each day when we set aside time to pray, meditate, and study, thereby bringing the Spirit into our lives and filling us with love for God and all his children. Sacred time can thus be a means of filling us with a desire to serve others and be more like him, as illustrated by the first two verses of the lovely hymn of William D. Longstaff (1822–1894), "Take Time to Be Holy":

> *Take time to be holy,*
> *Speak oft with thy Lord;*
> *Abide in Him always,*
> *And feed on His Word.*
> *Make friends of God's children,*
> *Help those who are weak,*
> *Forgetting in nothing*
> *His blessing to seek.*
>
> *Take time to be holy,*
> *The world rushes on;*
> *Spend much time in secret*
> *With Jesus alone;*
> *By looking to Jesus,*
> *Like Him thou shalt be;*
> *Thy friends in thy conduct*
> *His likeness shall see.*[2]

As we consider what the scriptures and the practices of other faith communities show us about the importance of sacred time, we can ask ourselves, How does taking time to be holy help us deepen our worship? How can deliberate use of sacred time help us set aside the world and break the usual flow of our activities? Why is the Sabbath about more than just what we do and don't do on Sundays? What is the role of memory and anticipation when it comes to celebrating holidays? How can we make them more Christ-centered? How can we make the regular aspects of our worship, such as daily prayer or scripture study, sacred time?

The Sabbath and Other Jewish Festivals

When Elaine and I were living in Philadelphia during graduate school, one of my fellow students and her husband invited us to their apartment for Friday dinner. Ellen and Michael were Jewish—he from a modern orthodox family, she from a secular family but newly observant—so in addition to looking forward to sharing a meal with friends I was also eager to share the start of the Sabbath with them. When Elaine and I arrived the apartment was clean, the meal was cooked, and the table was set and adorned with fresh flowers, all to welcome the Sabbath.

I do not remember what we ate that night or anything about the conversation. What I do remember is the prayers, said in Hebrew but carefully explained by our friends. Michael intoned the prayer over the braided ḥallah bread and then the cup of wine (they provided us with grape juice). But what I remember most was Ellen's lighting and blessing the Sabbath candles. Something magical seemed to happen at that moment, and I felt the kind of anticipation I do on Christmas morning. Suddenly we were transported to a different time and place, marked off from the rest of the world. It was Sabbath.

The daily cycle of time was recognized by the Israelites through the pattern of thrice-daily prayer, showing that time should be taken to recognize and commune with God as the day began, as it continued, and as it finally ended (Psalm 55:17; Daniel 6:10).[3] But the most significant cycle in the Old Testament was the weekly cycle that emphasized creation, completion, and renewal—the Sabbath. In many ways, the

Sabbath serves as a paradigm for all other sacred time, vividly illustrating what it means to take a day, a holiday, or an occasion, and then by keeping it holy create what Rabbi Hayim Donin called "an island in time."[4] Understanding the scriptural roots of our observance of sacred time can better help us take time to be holy on Sundays, holidays, and those moments throughout each day when we turn to God and create temporal space for worship.

When the Lord completed his creative labors on the sixth day, he blessed and sanctified the seventh (Genesis 2:2), indicating from the beginning that this was a sacred time. Reflecting its origin, our word *Sabbath* comes from the Hebrew *šābat*, the basic meaning of which is "to stop or cease."[5] The Sabbath was enshrined as a day of rest and worship in the law of Moses, particularly in the Ten Commandments (Exodus 20:8–11; see also Deuteronomy 5:12–15). The law's strong prohibitions against work and strict penalties for infractions set the Sabbath clearly apart from the rest of the week, something we seek to do today by refraining from unnecessary work and modifying our recreational and other activities. Besides providing a needed day of physical and mental rest, weekly observance of the Sabbath also helped the Israelites recognize how God had delivered them from bondage and had brought them into covenant with him.[6] This recognition makes our weekly focus on how Jesus has delivered us from the bondage of sin and death and our renewal of covenants through the sacrament particularly appropriate on our Sabbath.

Both ancient and modern observance of the Sabbath has sometimes focused on ceasing our usual labors and activities to enjoy a day of rest, but it can and should be more than that. President Spencer W. Kimball (1895–1985), twelfth president of the Church, taught that we should be actively engaged in doing uplifting, spiritual activities: "The Sabbath is a holy day in which to do worthy and holy things. Abstinence from work and recreation is important but insufficient. The Sabbath calls for constructive thoughts and acts, and if one merely lounges about doing nothing on the Sabbath, he is breaking it."[7]

SACRED TIME

I have found that taking time to be grateful is another important part of the spiritual heritage of the Sabbath. Because the primary significance of the seventh day was to commemorate God's completion of the Creation, one of the reasons we keep a Sabbath day and worship on it is to recognize God for his greatness and goodness, particularly in providing this beautiful and rich world for us to live in.[8] This aspect of the Sabbath sometimes eludes us, but as I think back on my father's sometimes lengthy prayers of thanks at Sunday dinner, I realize that our best meal of the week, served with ample helpings of gratitude, was actually a celebration of creation and all God's gifts to us. Perhaps also overlooked are the anticipatory aspects of the Sabbath, which parallel our looking forward to the promised Millennium, a time of peace, prosperity, and rest from war, strife, and sickness (Isaiah 11:5–9; 65:17–25).

In addition to the weekly Sabbath, the law of Moses established annual festivals to remember and celebrate God's deliverance of the children of Israel in the past and emphasize his continuing goodness to them. These feasts included Passover (Hebrew, *pesaḥ*), which celebrated their deliverance from Egypt; Festival of Weeks (Hebrew, *šābū'ôṯ*), which commemorated God's giving of the Law at Sinai; and Tabernacles (Hebrew, *sukkôt*), which recalled how God had sustained his people in the wilderness. After the wilderness wanderings, however, the Israelites also connected these three holidays with the agricultural rhythms of the Holy Land, associating them with the barley, wheat, and autumn harvests respectively.[9] They became pilgrimage festivals when people would take their first fruits to the temple in Jerusalem to celebrate together and thank the Lord for his bounty to them, much as we do at Thanksgiving and some other holidays.

The holiest days of the year, however, recognized God as Creator and Redeemer. Rosh Hashānāh, or the Jewish New Year, came to be seen as "the birthday of the world" and, like the weekly Sabbath, recognized the Creation.[10] On the other hand, Yôm Kippūr, or the Day of Atonement, looked forward to the world's judgment and ultimate redemption. As part of this atonement each year, the high priest performed a number of special sacrifices while the people were commanded to "afflict their souls" (Leviticus 16:29). This afflicting of souls was interpreted as fasting, which set Yôm Kippūr apart from daily life in a powerful way, signaling not only sorrow for sin but a desire to put the things of the Lord before all else.[11] Both of these ideas continue in our weekly Sunday Sabbath, as we come to church repentant and seeking to start the week anew by focusing on the atoning sacrifice of Jesus Christ.

From Sabbath to the Lord's Day

Jesus taught, "The sabbath was made for man, and not man for the sabbath" (Mark 2:27). When Rachel was little, Elaine and I were hesitant to teach her about keeping the Sabbath holy by emphasizing too much what we could and couldn't do on Sundays. As I strained to think of a way to teach her the principle without making a list of prohibitions, I was struck by a cute expression she had when she was three or four. To her, the name "Jesus" effectively meant anything holy or religious. Hence the scriptures were "the Jesus book" and the meetinghouse was "the Jesus house." So when the time came for a lesson on Sabbath observance, we decided to explain that Sunday was the "Jesus Day."

While it is true that we ended up making a list, it was a list of things that Rachel came up with that made her feel closer to the Lord, as well as a few things to avoid that didn't help her think of him. Our list has changed over the years, but the essential principle of guiding where we go, what we do, what we watch, and how we spend time on the Lord's Day by what helps us feel the Spirit has always felt right.

As a practicing Jew, Jesus observed sacred time by keeping all of the traditional Jewish festivals. All four Gospels record that he went up to Jerusalem for the last Passover of his mortal life, and the Gospel of John portrays him as participating in a number of festivals, demonstrating by his words and deeds that he fulfilled much of the symbolism of those festivals. For instance, his miraculous feeding the five thousand and walking on water are combined with his Bread of Life discourse to show that he was the same *YHWH*, or Jehovah, who had delivered and sustained the children of Israel in the wilderness and that he was now the "bread which came down from heaven" to sustain them spiritually (John 6:41).

The weekly Sabbath, however, is the sacred time that appears the most often in the mortal ministry of Jesus. Jesus was frequently found in Jewish synagogues reading and teaching on the Sabbath, but he also healed and cast out evil spirits while there. These healings were problematic to the Jews because Jesus was seen as a successful faith healer, so these activities were seen as his work. Taken together with the sometimes unconventional behavior of his disciples, such as their picking grain on the Sabbath, such activities led to charges that Jesus and his followers were Sabbath breakers (Mark 2:23–24; parallels Matthew 12:1–2; Luke 6:1–2). Jesus responded with one of his most important teachings about the Sabbath: "The sabbath was made for man, and not man for the sabbath: Therefore the Son of man is Lord also of the sabbath" (Mark 2:27–28). Here the Lord emphasizes that the Sabbath is meant to help uplift and inspire us, not for us to be constrained with burdensome rules of our own making. Indeed, beyond simply resting and worshipping, Jesus taught that we ought to seek to do good on the Sabbath (Mark 3:4; Luke 6:9; 14:5).[12] Moreover, the Sabbath should be focused on Jesus, the Lord of the Sabbath. In the story of healing the bent woman who was freed from her long infirmity and subsequently praised God, Jesus underscored that the Sabbath was about deliverance and praise (Luke 13:10–17). As *YHWH* he had delivered Israel from captivity, as the mortal Jesus he freed the woman from her infirmity, and as the risen Lord he will free us from sin and death.[13]

Initially Jewish Christians seem to have continued to observe the seventh day of the week as their Sabbath. Paul often attended the synagogue on the Sabbath, taking the opportunity to preach that Jesus was Israel's promised Messiah (Acts 13:14, 27, 42–44; 15:21; 16:13). When the Jerusalem Council met to determine which elements of the law of Moses should apply to Gentile Christians (Acts 15:6–29), it did not address whether the Sabbath or any of the other Jewish holidays should still be observed. Nor does the New Testament directly record the annual celebration of any important Christian commemorations, such as Christmas or Easter. Colossians 2:16, however, warned Christians not to judge each other in such matters as what we eat or which holy days or sabbaths we observe. Noting that the roots of the Sabbath go to the Creation, well before the law of Moses, biblical scholar Daniel Block observed, "It seems more important *that a Sabbath day be observed* than *which Sabbath day is observed.*"[14]

Early Christians soon began observing the Sabbath on the first day of the week. Because the first day of the week was the day Jesus rose triumphantly from the tomb, Sunday became known as the Lord's Day. Acts 20:7–11 records that Paul broke bread, presumably as part of the sacrament, with the Saints at Troas on the first day of the week, and John the Revelator notes that he had a powerful vision of the risen Lord on the Lord's Day (Revelation 1:10).[15] For us as well, Sunday is an appropriate time for us to come together each week to remember how Jesus suffered and died and then on the first day of the week rose again, making every Sunday a commemoration of Easter. While the seventh day had symbolized the creation of the old world, the first day now represented the beginning of a new creation. The new Sabbath's rest thus looks forward to the eternal rest that we will obtain in heaven, giving new meaning to Jesus' words, "Come unto me, all ye that labour and are heavy laden, and I will give you rest" (Matthew 11:28).[16]

The spiritual rebirth we have had in Christ, the peace we enjoy in him now, and the promised eternal peace we have been promised give our Sunday Sabbath new and powerful meaning, which, if carefully observed and celebrated, brings a powerful spirit into our lives. But we should not limit our time with the Savior to once a week. As William Longstaff noted, we should take time for this every day, in every situation:

> *Take time to be holy,*
> *Let Him be thy guide.*
> *And run not before Him*
> *Whatever betide.*

SACRED TIME

In joy or in sorrow
Still follow the Lord,
And, looking to Jesus,
Still trust in His Word.[17]

Sacred Time among Jews, Christians, and Muslims

As Latter-day Saints we are generally good about keeping the Sabbath holy, at least for the most part. We certainly know how to celebrate Christmas, though perhaps we need to work harder at keeping Christ at the center of it. But sometimes other possibilities for sacred time escape us. I have certainly learned a lot in this regard from my Jewish and Muslim friends and from Christians of other faiths.

When my family and I lived in Jerusalem, we attended our Church meetings on Saturday, the day on which Latter-day Saints in the Holy Land observe the Sabbath. That practice freed us to visit many other churches for their services on Sundays. The highlights of these visits were services in the English-speaking Lutheran or Anglican churches in the Old City at the various holidays of the Christian liturgical year. I had read about Holy Week services, Easter sunrise services, and Advent Sunday services, but this was the first time I was able to attend them.

When we returned to Provo and Easter was approaching, Rachel asked me, "Where are we going for Holy Week services?" Taking the challenge, I found the schedule for St. Mary's Episcopal Church in Provo. Three days before Easter we joined a small congregation in that lovely church for its Maundy Thursday service. Hearing the story of the Last Supper and Jesus' prayer in the garden read aloud as part of a traditional service touched me and made me think more deeply of what the Lord did for me that night. It made me think of sacred time and how it can help us remember the most important events in the history of the world.

The ways our friends of other faiths mark sacred time and celebrate holidays can remind us of the importance of taking time to be holy ourselves. When observing a weekly Sabbath, attending weekly services, or celebrating religious holidays, Jews, Christians, and Muslims have developed ways of preparing for sacred time, of behaving during it, and of being changed after it that can encourage us to be more deliberate and mindful in our own worship.

Rabbinic Judaism, for instance, developed many traditions that have made their Sabbath, which begins at sundown on Friday and ends at sunset on Saturday, the focus of religious life both in the home and in the synagogue.[18] Families prepare for it as if preparing to welcome an honored guest by cleaning the home, dressing in their best clothes, and preparing a lovely meal. Families gather around the table to usher in the Sabbath eve by the lighting of two special candles, blessing loaves of *ḥallah* and cups of ceremonial wine, and singing joyfully.[19] In the synagogue a special prayer service exuberantly welcomes the Sabbath with psalms and singing Friday evening, and further services are held the next morning. After spending leisure time outside these services with their families and studying Jewish texts, many Jews gather Saturday evening to conclude the Sabbath together with a special prayer and ceremony,[20] thereby marking the close of sacred time and invoking the Lord's blessings as they move forward into the new week. We have a similar two-fold tradition of honoring the Sabbath at home and at church, but I find that my honoring of the Sabbath is deeper when I make an extra effort to prepare for Sunday. Personally I have found that formally opening the Sabbath in my personal and family prayers and then closing it with pleas for the Lord to bless us with his Spirit in the coming week increases the day's effect.

Jewish tradition has also increased the impact of their observance of holidays with special prayer services, specific music, traditional foods, and other customs meant to help reinforce what each holiday represents and to highlight its difference from ordinary time. Even sad commemorations, like the annual Fast of Tisha b'Av, which marks the destructions of the ancient temples and other disasters that have befallen the Jewish people, or set periods of mourning after the death of loved ones, are important uses of time.[21] On the other hand, important joyful holidays are set apart from ordinary time by beginning them with the recitation of a customary blessing known as the *sheheḥeyānû*, which means "who has given us life":

> *Blessed art Thou, O Lord our God, King of the
> Universe, who has given us life and sustained
> us and enabled us to reach this season.*²²

Similarly, almost all of our own families have beloved traditions, foods, and decorations that mark our own holidays and make those times special. In addition, our family has developed the practice of trying to be more deliberate about preparing for and celebrating our holidays. For instance, as we decorate in the weeks before Christmas and Easter, we often have a special family home evening discussion about the symbolism of our decorations and customs, express thanks for the joyous time we are entering, and pray for the special spirit of that season to fill our home.

The most important feature of traditional Christianity's weekly Sunday observance is the weekly celebration of the Eucharist, when Christians come together to pray, sing, hear scriptural lessons recited, and, above all, receive the sacrament of the Lord's Supper.²³ The development of the Christian liturgical calendar emphasized holidays great and small throughout the year. The most important of these was Easter,²⁴ the celebration of which quickly expanded in the fourth century, commemorating not only Jesus' resurrection but also all the events leading up to it in what came to be known as Holy Week. The beginning of much of this celebration began in Jerusalem, where sacred time and holy places converged as pilgrims began the custom of retracing Jesus' final steps and days, beginning with the triumphal entry on Palm Sunday and continuing with the events of his final night in mortality on Thursday and the day of his death on Good Friday.²⁵ Although Latter-day Saints do not formally observe any of these holidays beyond special sacrament meeting programs on Easter Sunday, using sacred time to commemorate what Jesus did for us by reading about these events from the scriptures and perhaps studying them and celebrating them as families can provide powerful opportunities for individual worship.

Celebrations of the Christmas season similarly evolved. After initially celebrating Jesus' birth in the spring, by the fourth century

Christians had settled on December 25, a date associated with the winter solstice, which produced a joyful midwinter festival that celebrated the arrival of the Light of the World at the darkest time of the year.[26] To better prepare for the annual commemoration of Jesus' birth, Pope Gregory the Great (A.D. 590–604) established Advent, four weeks of solemn preparation that helped worshippers see how the Old Testament prophecies of Christ were about to be fulfilled. A multiplication of holy days ensued, commemorating not just the various events of Jesus' life but also the lives, and particularly the martyrdoms, of Christian saints.[27]

Islam also developed daily, weekly, and annual cycles of time meant to create times for worshippers to remember God and submit to him. Formal ritual prayer, or *ṣalāt*, five times each day constantly reminds Muslims of their duty to God. Their week is marked by the obligation to join in communal ritual prayer each Friday afternoon (Arabic, *Jumu'ah*) and then listen to a sermon by the *imām*, or prayer leader.[28] For Muslims the most important sacred time is the holy month of Ramaḍān, the ninth month in the Islamic lunar calendar, which commemorates the revelation of the holy Qur'ān to Muḥammad. Observing Ramaḍān is one of the Five Pillars of Islam, marked by dawn-to-dusk fasting the entire month. Whereas in Judaism fasting is primarily a way of mourning or showing contrition, for Muslims fasting focuses the worshipper on spiritual rather than on physical needs, much as it does for Latter-day Saints. In the context of Ramaḍān, fasting also symbolizes being fed by God's word, so during this holy month many Muslims strive to read the entire Qur'ān.

The Protestant Reformation saw a certain limiting of sacred time in an attempt to stay closer to the biblical model. Martin Luther, John Wesley, and other reformers eliminated numerous saints' days and other holidays.[29] Still, some Protestant denominations—such as Lutherans and Anglicans and to a lesser extent Methodists and Presbyterians—retained the basic aspects of the Christian liturgical year, seeing in such observances as Advent and Holy Week effective ways of helping worshippers better prepare themselves for Christmas and Easter. Others, however, stripped the calendar of anything not mentioned in the Bible, which meant that some Puritans and Anabaptists chose not even to celebrate Christmas. On the other hand, Calvinists and Puritans kept Sunday as the Sabbath and observed it with rigor, often imposing community punishments on Sabbath breakers.[30] The earliest Latter-day Saints, many coming from a New England background, certainly honored the Sabbath and observed Christmas and Easter somewhat more moderately.

Sacred Time in the Restoration

Years ago I read the following in President Gordon B. Hinckley's Christmas message: "There would be no Christmas if there had not been Easter. The babe Jesus of Bethlehem would be but another baby without the redeeming Christ of Gethsemane and Calvary, and the triumphant fact of the Resurrection."[31] That message changed the way I have celebrated Christmas and Easter ever since.

Over the years our family has developed new traditions for the holidays based on this premise. The teachings of the Restoration have deepened our understanding of who Jesus is and what he came to do for us. Weaving together traditional observances, biblical and Restoration scripture, music, and testimony, we have tried to make holidays sacred time, using the four weeks before Christmas and the week before Easter for daily family devotionals that focus our minds and hearts on what these holidays are all about.[32]

Each individual and family approaches sacred time differently. Sacred time is more than just going to church on Sundays. It is finding time to worship and employing memory to better seek, and find, God and then letting him transform us.

The organization meeting of the Church on April 6, 1830—complete with baptisms, the sacrament of the Lord's Supper, confirmations, and ordinations—was on a Tuesday. The first Church conference, held on June 9, 1830, however, was on a Sunday, and given their New England Protestant backgrounds, early members of the Church naturally observed the Sabbath on the first day of the week.[33] Later, on August 7, 1831, a revelation provided the Restoration mandate for worshipping weekly on Sunday; this revelation also established that one of the primary ways we keep the Sabbath is by meeting together and partaking of the sacrament (D&C 59:9–13). Indeed, the remission of sins and the companionship of the Spirit we seek is the ultimate rest that the Lord has promised us, making the rest from our daily labors and concerns a type of the peace and eternal rest we are anticipating in the celestial kingdom.[34]

Throughout its history, the Church has received counsel from its leaders to better observe the Sabbath, who emphasize that above all the Sabbath should be a sacred time focused on worship.[35] For this practice to be effective, both leaders and members alike must be deliberate in their planning and personal preparation. With recent direction from Church leadership for ward councils to work closely with bishoprics to improve our Sunday meetings, especially our sacrament meetings,[36] leaders should seek direction from the Spirit. President Boyd K. Packer taught, "Our sacrament and other meetings need renewed attention to assure that they are truly worship services in which members may be spiritually nourished and have their testimonies replenished."[37]

As Moroni taught regarding worship among his own people, "And their meetings were conducted by the church after the manner of the workings of the Spirit, and by the power of the Holy Ghost; for as the power of the Holy Ghost led them whether to preach, or to exhort, or to pray, or to supplicate, or to sing, even so it was done" (Moroni 6:9). Much of this direction can, and should, come in the planning beforehand, but those presiding also have the right to receive inspiration regarding any changes they should make even in the course of a meeting. As members, on the other hand, we should prepare ourselves so that we can feel the Spirit as we speak, listen, pray, sing, or participate in ordinances. As we shall see, careful and frequent use of scripture and music are particularly potent means of bringing the Spirit into our Sabbath meetings as well as into our family and personal worship.

The pointed counsel of Elder Mark E. Petersen (1900–1984), a member of the Twelve, regarding the focus of our Sabbath worship is helpful in seeing how the risen Lord should be the focus both of our meetings and of our other Sabbath day activities: "We can readily see that observance of the Sabbath is an indication of the depth of our conversion. Our observance or nonobservance of the Sabbath is an unerring measure of our attitude toward the Lord personally and toward his suffering in Gethsemane, his death on the cross, and his resurrection from the dead."[38]

In terms of intentionality in planning and executing our meetings, Elder Petersen's injunction means that we should strive to emulate Nephi's declaration when he said, "We talk of Christ, we rejoice in Christ, we preach of Christ, we prophesy of Christ, and we write according to our prophecies, that our children may know to what source they may look for a remission of their sins" (2 Nephi 25:26). Any subject of a sacrament sermon or a class lesson can, and should, be tied to Jesus Christ and his saving work. If that is the case, then we are promised the confirming presence of the Holy Ghost, which makes listening to the talk or participating in the lesson an act of worship.

Likewise, emphasis on the Savior and his gospel should be the focus of our family and individual Sabbath activities outside our Church meetings. Like our Jewish friends, we can set the entire Sabbath apart from the rest of the week by how we dress, what we eat, the music we listen to, the activities we engage in, and with whom we spend it. In ideal circumstances, much of this will be done with our families, but the principle applies even if we find ourselves alone on the Sabbath.[39] Over time, Church leaders have made many good suggestions and given specific direction on what we should and should not do on the Sabbath—such as avoiding unnecessary work, shopping, and recreation on Sundays.[40] As President Russell M. Nelson, president of the Council of the Twelve Apostles since July 2015, taught, ultimately our conduct and our attitude on the Sabbath represents a sign between us and God: "With that understanding, I no longer needed lists of dos and don'ts. When I had to make a decision whether or not an activity was appropriate for the Sabbath, I simply asked myself, 'What sign do

I want to give to God?'"[41] With this touchstone question in mind, we can make individual choices according to whether they take us closer to our goal of encountering and being transformed by God in this period of sacred time. We can then indeed "call the sabbath a delight" (Isaiah 58:13).

The practice of fasting creates another kind of sacred time in the Restoration. In today's Church, fasting is normally practiced by abstaining from food and drink for two meals, usually twenty-four hours, with the money saved being donated to the needy through fast offerings. Fasting is effective when it is done with a purpose and intention clearly in mind as the focus of prayer.[42] In the early Church a fast and testimony meeting was held on the first Thursday of the month in conjunction with this fast, providing participants an opportunity to share testimony while they were in the heightened spiritual state created by fasting and the concentrated prayer that ought to accompany it. In 1896 this meeting was changed to the first Sunday of the month.[43]

Whether done with other members as part of the monthly fast or as a voluntary, individual fast at another time, fasting marks a sacred period of time when we open and close our fasts with prayer. We can use the time of the fast to increase our prayerfulness and focus on the purpose for which we are fasting. Sometimes we may fast for comfort in times of sorrow or as part of repentance, as the Jewish tradition does. Other times we may fast as an aid to prayer for a particular need or purpose. Together with our Muslim friends, I am drawn to the idea of fasting as time to concentrate on spiritual matters rather than on physical needs, to rejoice in the word of the Lord, and to draw closer to God. This desire for God is beautifully illustrated in Psalm 42: "As the hart panteth after the water brooks, so panteth my soul after thee, O God. My soul thirsteth for God, for the living God: when shall I come and appear before God?" (Psalm 42:1–2). As we hunger and thirst for the Lord during the sacred time of our fasting, he feeds us with his word and blesses us with the presence of his Spirit, as illustrated by the chorus of John S. Tanner's hymn, "Bless Our Fast, We Pray":

> *Feed thou our souls, fill thou our hearts,*
> *And bless our fast, we pray.*
> *That we may feel thy presence here*
> *And feast with thee today.*[44]

Though Latter-day Saints do not follow the traditional Christian liturgical calendar with its many set holidays, we have developed a particular love for Christmas. We do not hold formal church services on Christmas Eve or on Christmas morning (except when one of these falls on a Sunday), but the sacrament meeting closest to Christmas is usually dedicated to celebrating the birth of Jesus Christ. Such meetings can be particularly moving when ample scripture and music accompany the assigned talks. The First Presidency's Christmas Devotional has become the Church Christmas devotional featuring inspired talks and stirring music from the Mormon Tabernacle Choir and Orchestra at Temple Square. By far, however, most of the sacred time of the Christmas season is celebrated in the home by families. A Christ-centered Christmas requires effort and intent to stand above the commercial and cultural tides that sweep around it in our society. But if celebrated thoughtfully, Christmas can be a wonderful teaching opportunity, bringing not just our children but ourselves closer to the Savior through the considered use of scripture, music, and prayer through the broader season leading up to Christmas day.

If it were not for cultural and commercial considerations that have made the Christmas season so widely celebrated, Easter would certainly be the more important of these two holidays. As it is, many Latter-day Saints often find themselves still striving to make Easter a more sacred time. As a holiday that falls on a different date each year, it is a shifting target that sometimes makes planning difficult for ward leadership. Yet as bishoprics and ward councils work at improving Sunday worship generally, they have a prime opportunity to make Easter Sunday a spiritual feast through the same means we use with ward Christmas sacrament meetings: carefully chosen scripture readings, wonderful music, and appropriate talks full of testimony.

When I was a young bishop, we used the Christmas template in our efforts to deepen our devotion at Easter, filling the chapel with flowers and using Easter music and topics in the weeks leading up to Easter. But as with Christmas, making Easter a sacred time when we can really find God, come to know Jesus Christ better, and be transformed by what he has done for us is largely a personal and family effort. Using the scriptural accounts of the Savior's final days as the subject of family and personal scripture study in the week leading up to Easter can be particularly effective. For years now our family has held special family devotionals each evening from Palm Sunday through Easter with special attention to Maundy Thursday and Good Friday so that we can remember what Jesus did for us on those days.

Holidays mark weekly, monthly, and yearly rhythms in life and provide sacred moments. So do other daily patterns in our practice of family and personal prayer and weekly family home evening. These occasions are not always spiritually momentous; in fact, if we are not careful, they can become routine. But even the routines of weekly family home evenings and daily family prayer and scripture study will yield a lifetime of rewards if done regularly. As Elder David A. Bednar of the Twelve observed, what is important is the consistency that brings the Spirit into our lives and allows such patterns of worship to change us:

"Each family prayer, each episode of family scripture study, and each family home evening is a brushstroke on the canvas of our souls. No one event may appear to be very impressive or memorable. But just as the yellow and gold and brown strokes of paint complement each other and produce an impressive masterpiece, so our consistency in doing seemingly small things can lead to significant spiritual results."[45]

Consistency and intent yield similar fruit in our personal devotions. If we begin each instance of individual prayer, scripture reading, reflection, and other devotions with an understanding that we are taking time to be with God in those moments, seek his Spirit, and focus our attention solely on him, we will create regular, meaningful space for worship.

In addition, births, baptisms, priesthood ordinations and Young Women achievements, mission calls, marriages, and funerals are rites of passage in which God can be truly present if we plan them intentionally and seek to feel his Spirit in celebrating them. William Longstaff wrote:

> *Take time to be holy,*
> *Be calm in thy soul,*
> *Each thought and each motive*
> *Beneath His control;*
>
> *Thus led by His Spirit*
> *To fountains of love,*
> *Thou soon shalt be fitted*
> *For service above.*[46]

The transformation that occurs when we take time to be holy does more than allow us to go forth to serve God and others with all our strength in this life. Such worship fits us for eternal service in heaven.

READING, PREACHING, AND TEACHING GOD'S WORD

Discovering God While Feasting upon His Word

> *Thy words were found, and I did eat them;*
> *and thy word was unto me the joy*
> *and rejoicing of mine heart:*
> *for I am called by thy name, O Lord God of hosts.*
> —Jeremiah 15:16

> *Wherefore, he that preacheth and he that receiveth, understand one another, and both are edified and rejoice together.*
> —Doctrine & Covenants 50:22

Communing with God by feeling his Spirit is a primary goal in worship, and such communion is always greatest when he speaks back to us in some way. Without minimizing the importance of direct contact through revelation, visions, and dreams, we can safely say that the most common way that we hear the Lord is through his word, both as it has come to us through the scriptures and as we receive it from hearing those who are inspired.[1] Jeremiah wrote of finding the words of God and then eating them, an image found also in Ezekiel's experience in eating a scroll from God which tasted sweet to him (Jeremiah 15:16; Ezekiel 3:1). The powerful metaphor of feasting upon the word of Christ is also found in the Book of Mormon, where feasting seems to connote not just eating for spiritual sustenance but also doing it eagerly, even joyfully. If we endure to the end while regularly and enthusiastically partaking of the word of God, we will obtain eternal life; while yet in this life, the words of Christ will direct us how to live (2 Nephi 31:20; 32:3).

As a result, it is natural to turn to the scriptures before, after, and even during prayer to find in their pages what the Lord is saying to us. Bryan Chappell, president of the Covenant Theological Seminary, observed, "Reading the Word of God becomes the very core of worship, affording each hearer an opportunity for ongoing, personal encounter with the divine."[2] The scriptures also deepen the experiences we have with ordinances, explaining these sacred acts and their significance and adding to the spirit we feel as we participate in them. Reading the scriptures creates space for worship—temporally, mentally, and spiritually—as we step aside from the world to look for, and find, the will of God. When the scriptures are the foundation of our teaching, they invite the Spirit into our services and classes, allowing God to speak through us and to us as we speak and listen (D&C 50:22). But the word of God is not limited just to canonized texts; we find it in the inspired teaching of our leaders and even in each other's words when the spirit is present as we study and worship together.

Feasting upon the word is a deliberate act: it does not happen just by casually reading, speaking, or listening. It requires that we intentionally consider what we read, say, and hear, understanding that it is coming from God. Mindfulness in such feasting requires that we be open to what the Spirit is saying to us, setting aside both doubts and preconceived notions. In short, to qualify as worship, feasting upon the word requires concentration and intention, what our Jewish friends call *kavanah,* and not just mere reading or hearing.

As we worship through the word of God, how can the love we feel for him and the respect we feel for his word deepen our experience? How do we discover God and his will for us in the pages of the scriptures? What is the difference between just reading and feasting upon the word? What role can the scriptures play in preparing us for prayer and finding answers in them? What can we learn from other faith traditions about valuing them and studying them? Finally, how can we better incorporate the scriptures into our family worship and our church classes and meetings?

Teaching Priests, Preaching Prophets, and Inspired Poets in the Hebrew Bible

Ne'ot Kedumim, meaning "pleasant pastures of old," is a Biblical Landscape Park in Israel that recreates the ancient settings of the Bible.[3] It is filled with the plants and animals mentioned in the Old Testament, and it includes other features such as wells, threshing floors, and olive and wine presses. While living in Jerusalem, we would take our BYU-Jerusalem students there every semester so that they could better picture the stories that we were reading about in our religion classes.

At the end of each tour of the biblical park, we were treated to a special demonstration of how a Torah scribe faithfully copies that sacred text onto a new scroll using parchment and ink prepared from local products according to Jewish law. The scribe explained that he immersed himself in a ritual *miqveh* bath and recited blessings to ceremonially prepare himself for his sacred work each day. He then showed us how he carefully copied the Torah letter by letter and then ensured its accuracy by counting letters and carefully comparing it to other scrolls. He also explained that he repeated another blessing each time he wrote the sacred name of God. As we watched him work, we realized that copying the sacred texts was more than a labor of love—it was an act of worship.

Although Restoration scripture informs us that the earliest prophets and patriarchs kept a book of remembrance in which they recorded their inspiration and revelation (Moses 6:5, 46), except for what has been restored in the Pearl of Great Price, we do not have any of those texts. Instead, the oldest records in our current Old Testament are the books attributed to Moses, the writings by and about the Hebrew prophets, and various books of inspired poetry and other literature. Together these writings constitute the Jewish scriptures that the earliest Christians adopted and handed down to us. The different kinds of books in the Old Testament illustrate how the scriptures teach us about God's commandments, reveal his will to us, and inspire and encourage us. They also show us how his servants continue to guide us in these same ways today.

The compositional and editorial history of the first five books of the Bible—Genesis, Exodus, Leviticus, Numbers, and Deuteronomy—is complex and much debated, but by tradition they are attributed to Moses, who is the prophet and central figure in much of them.[4] These five books came to be known as the Pentateuch, "five scrolls," when they were translated into Greek, but in Hebrew they are known as the Torah. Although often rendered as "the Law," *tôrāh* more accurately means "teaching" or "instruction."[5] In addition to legal material (Hebrew, *halākāh*), Torah includes historical narratives, poetic songs, genealogies, and other material.[6] It thus embraces not just the detailed aspects of the law of Moses but everything that the Lord teaches us from the lives of the early prophets and patriarchs to the experiences of the children of Israel in the wilderness.[7] References to the Lord's law are woven throughout much of the Bible, especially in the Psalms, where the law of the Lord is referred to by such words as "statutes," "ordinances," and "precepts."[8]

When the Israelites gathered at the foot of Mount Sinai, Moses ascended to receive the Lord's law. Bringing it down, he instructed the Israelites regarding the will of *YHWH,* or Jehovah, and put them under covenant (Exodus 19–24). In this way, Moses was an anticipation and a type of Jesus Christ, who more fully revealed God's will and taught the gospel to us (Deuteronomy 18:15). Towards the end of his ministry, the Bible records, Moses wrote down key parts of the law and instructed the priests that they should regularly read it to the people (Deuteronomy 31:9–12; 33:8–11). As a priest who teaches (2 Chronicles 15:3), such a servant of the Lord was to teach the people the word of the Lord so they would know how to keep the covenant,[9] much as our Latter-day Saint leaders, at both the general and the local level, ensure that we know the laws and principles of the gospel and encourage us to keep the commandments today.

In addition to teaching the people through priests, God sent prophets to preach his word. In Hebrew, a prophet was a *nābî'*, "a spokesperson." As a result, although a prophet could proclaim future events, his primary function was to be a "forth-teller," one who proclaimed God's will, not a "foreteller."[10] Frequently employing poetic and heavily symbolic language, the Hebrew prophets addressed God's word to the current situation of the people, called them to repentance, warned of the consequences for disobedience, and promised future redemption and restoration. Many prophecies also anticipated and foretold details of the person and work of Jesus Christ (Jacob 4:4).

The prophecies and stories about the prophets were written down and preserved, often by themselves but sometimes by others. Together these prophecies and stories constitute another principal section of the Hebrew Bible, namely the *Nebî'îm*, "the Prophets." The historical books from Joshua through 2 Kings, whose authors are unknown, are included in this section because by later tradition important prophets were believed to have compiled them.[11] Reading and learning from the prophetic and historical books with the Spirit provides us important opportunities to "liken all scriptures unto us, that it might be for our profit and learning" (1 Nephi 19:23). They also provide a model for how modern prophets and apostles guide, direct, and encourage us today.

In addition to revealing his word to his prophets, God also inspired poets and other writers to create evocative and didactic texts known as the *Ketûbîm*, "Writings."[12] Most of these were compiled and edited after the Jews returned from the Babylonian exile, which began in 539 B.C., when the period of active prophets was drawing to a close. As a result, later Jewish scribes believed that they contained God's word to a lesser degree than did the *Nebî'îm* (the Prophets). Prominent in the Writings section of the Hebrew Bible are such poetic books as the Psalms, which provide powerful expressions of praise that are still used for worship by both Jews and Christians alike. Proverbs, Ecclesiastes, and Job are poetic books classified as wisdom literature because they are inspired treatments of important life questions, such as why there is evil in the world and why the righteous suffer. A later historian known as the Chronicler composed a secondary history covering some of the same material as First and Second Kings and likely assembled the records of Nehemiah and Ezra. Also appearing in the Writings is the book of Daniel, which, despite containing oracles and stories of the earlier prophet, was compiled considerably later, after the return from the Babylonian exile. Other gifted writers produced such books as Ruth and Esther, using the stories of biblical heroines to teach important lessons. The Writings have a peculiar power to move and inspire people in every age,[13] reminding us we can find inspiration and wisdom in all good literature (D&C 88:118; 90:15; 109:7, 14).

It was after the return from exile that the Torah, the books of the prophets, and the growing body of other inspired writings were brought together to be regularly studied and taught as scripture. The pivotal figure in the process was Ezra, who is often known as "the scribe" because he collected the sacred records that had been written up to that time and caused them to become a central part of Jewish worship.[14] When Ezra returned to Jerusalem with the second wave of returning exiles about 458 B.C., he found the spiritual situation of the people there to be very grave. Gathering the people together, he read the Torah to them and had it carefully explained:

"And Ezra opened the book in the sight of all the people; (for he was above all the people;) and when he opened it, all the people stood up: and Ezra blessed the Lord, the great God. And all the people answered, Amen, Amen, with lifting up their hands: and *they bowed their heads, and worshipped the Lord with their faces to the ground.* . . . So they read in the book in the law of God distinctly, and gave the sense, and *caused them to understand the reading*" (Nehemiah 8:5–8; emphasis added).

When the people heard the word of God read, they responded with outward expressions of worship, and the combination of hearing the word and feeling the Spirit gave them understanding. In the centuries between Ezra and Jesus, reading, studying, and teaching the Torah, the Prophets, and the Writings became central ways of worshipping God, drawing his people closer to him, inspiring them, teaching them, and helping them live according to his law and covenants.

Proclaiming the Good News in the Greek New Testament

When I was in high school in Tennessee, I occasionally attended Sunday evening or Wednesday night worship services with my friends at the First Baptist Church of Jackson. The preacher was incredibly gifted and very skilled at moving the audience. This was a different style of preaching than what I was used to, and I was a bit skeptical at first, assuming that he was mostly playing on the congregation's emotions. But as I suspended judgment and opened my mind, I began to learn something. I did not agree with all of his interpretation of scripture or with some of the things he said, but when he preached "Jesus Christ, and him crucified" (1 Corinthians 2:2), I felt the familiar impress of the Spirit upon my heart. God is no respecter of persons, and everyone who will seek and testify of his Son can receive a witness of the essential gospel message that he sent Jesus to suffer, die, and rise again for us.

At the beginning of Jesus' ministry, soon after his forty-day period of preparation in the wilderness, he returned to his hometown of Nazareth and attended a service in the local synagogue. Following the pattern started with Ezra, he stood up to read a passage from scripture and then sat down and explained it.[15] The passage he read came from the scroll containing the book of Isaiah: "The Spirit of the Lord is upon me, *because he hath anointed me to preach the gospel to the poor;* he hath sent me to heal the brokenhearted, to preach deliverance to the captives, and recovering of sight to the blind, to set at liberty them that are bruised, *to preach the acceptable year of the Lord*" (Luke 4:18–19; emphasis added).

Jesus sat down and explained that this passage was fulfilled in his mission. Throughout his ministry, Jesus revealed a thorough familiarity with the Jewish scriptures, using them regularly in his teaching. In the Synoptic Gospels, for instance, he quoted from or alludes to all five books of the Torah, most of the Prophets, and several of the Writings.[16]

But Jesus did not just read the scriptures or teach from them.

Rather he frequently expanded upon them, as he did in the Sermon on the Mount, leading listeners to observe that "he taught them as one having authority, and not as the scribes" (Matthew 7:29). Although Jesus used the scriptures in his teaching, the Gospels depict him primarily as a prophetic preacher. Much of the Christian word of God was oral, being heard as preaching rather than being read. For instance, one of the opening scenes of Mark says, "Jesus came into Galilee, *preaching the gospel of the kingdom of God,* and saying, The time is fulfilled, and the kingdom of God is at hand: repent ye, and believe the gospel" (Mark 1:14–15; emphasis added). *Gospel* means "good news" (Greek, *euangellion*), and after the first Easter, the apostles preached this good news by focusing squarely on Jesus' vicarious suffering, saving death, and liberating resurrection.

This testimony of Jesus was not written as part of a narrative story of his ministry until later in the apostolic period, first with the Gospel according to Mark in the mid A.D. 60s, then with Matthew and Luke sometime in the 70s, and finally John as late as the 90s. Even before these Gospels were written, this post-Easter gospel was already at the heart of the apostolic preaching, as seen in the speeches of Peter and Paul in the book of Acts and in their own writings. The apostolic proclamation (Greek, *kērygma*), or testimony, consisted of the saving message that God had sent his Son, who went about doing good, died on the cross, rose from the dead, and ascended to heaven, from where he would return to save his people from the powers of the world.[17] Though we cannot hear Peter and Paul preach today, we can read their words, which can have a similar effect upon us. Likewise, today we can hear the testimonies of living apostles and prophets, who can speak with the same authority and the same power.

In his frequent use of the Jewish scriptures during his ministry, Jesus endorsed the three-fold division of the Jewish canon when, after his resurrection and shortly before his ascension, he said to his disciples, "These are the words which I spake unto you, while I was yet with you, that all things must be fulfilled, which were written in the law of Moses, and in the prophets, and in the psalms, *concerning me*" (Luke 24:44; emphasis added). These were the scriptures of the early Christians, and 2 Timothy indicates that they were used in a similar way:

"And that from a child thou hast known the holy scriptures, *which are able to make thee wise unto salvation through faith which is in Christ Jesus.* All scripture is given by inspiration of God, and is profitable for doctrine, for reproof, for correction, for instruction in righteousness: That the man of God may be perfect, throughly furnished unto all good works" (2 Timothy 3:15–17; emphasis added).

To the Jewish scriptures were soon added letters of the apostles and writings of other Church leaders, which were circulated and copied even before the Gospels were written. These were largely concerned with the doctrinal, behavioral, and life concerns of the congregations to which they were written,[18] but they still have meaning to us as we read them, compare our situations with those of the original audiences, and look for the lasting principles that they teach. These new books held the same position for early Christians as conference talks and printed First Presidency messages do for us today, reminding us that what our leaders "speak when moved upon by the Holy Ghost shall be scripture, shall be the will of the Lord, shall be the mind of the Lord, shall be the word of the Lord, shall be the voice of the Lord, and the power of God unto salvation" (D&C 68:4).

Scriptures and Preaching from Antiquity through the Restoration

Catholic, Lutheran, and Anglican services have a custom that I have always appreciated. After a reading from the Old Testament or one of the New Testament letters, the reader concludes by saying, "This is the word of the Lord," to which the congregation responds, "Thanks be to God!" I am impressed by how this simple response recognizes that the Bible is the word of God even as it expresses to him our gratitude for it. But my favorite part is how the reading from one of the Gospels is done. According to tradition, one of the church's deacons walks down and stands in the midst of the congregation, holding the text high so all can see it. Everyone stands to honor God's word about his

READING, PREACHING, AND TEACHING GOD'S WORD

Son Jesus and listens attentively. At times like this I am reminded how casual I can be sometimes about my own scripture reading.

The way other faith traditions value and use their sacred texts provides us with good models of how we deepen our use of our own scriptures in our worship. The texts are studied carefully, and even the books in which they are written or printed are treated with great respect because they represent the word of God. Religious services are focused on reading and preaching from them, making God's word to his people an important part of communal worship.

In the Jewish synagogue service that developed after the destruction of the temple in A.D. 70, public readings from both the Torah and the Prophets came to hold a central position. Other scriptures, such as Psalms, are also used for worship to express praise, and passages from other Writings are read on certain holidays. What sermons or preaching there may be focuses on expositions of the texts that have been read.[19] As the word of God, the Torah is deeply revered, as is made clear by the deep respect that is shown for the scrolls upon which it is written. Torah scrolls are stored in a special ark, or cabinet, brought out with considerable pomp, honored and decorated as if for a king, and read using a special pointer so that the text itself is not touched. When a scroll becomes worn out, it is never thrown away or burned. Rather, it is buried or stored in a special repository.

Outside the public readings in synagogue, the Torah has become the center of individual and group study. While prayer is termed "the service of the heart" in the Jewish tradition, study is the service of the mind and is seen as a way of having a conversation with God.[20] So real can his presence be when reading that a tradition holds that whenever a group of Jews studies the Law together, the presence of God is among them.[21] This idea of study as worship extended to important texts and commentaries that were composed after the Torah and the rest of the Hebrew Bible.[22] This love of God's law is powerfully illustrated in Psalm 119, which is a 176-verse poem celebrating the Torah. One of its

103

lines is particularly powerful: "How sweet are thy words unto my taste! yea, sweeter than honey to my mouth!" (Psalm 119:103). Sometimes to teach this point, a Jewish father will put a drop of honey on a young child's tongue when the scriptures are being read.[23] Infusing our children with a love of the scriptures from an early age, and cultivating it in ourselves, is a worthy goal we can emulate.

Public reading of scripture became a central part of Christian services and was a principal feature leading up to the celebration of the Eucharist. This was "the service of the word" and often included three readings, or lessons, one from the Old Testament, one from the New Testament epistles, and one from the Gospels.[24] The prominent role of these readings made the service a two-fold experience of worship: the people came before God and prayed to him; they received his response, first through his Word and second through the gift of his Son in the form of the bread and wine of the Eucharist. To these readings was added the preaching of a homily, or sermon, based upon one of the scriptural lessons, a practice that became important because of the example of John Chrysostom (c. A.D. 349–407), a bishop of Constantinople who was famous for his preaching. Chrysostom's pulpit was often the same lectern or reading desk from which the scripture had just been read, emphasizing that his sermon was an exposition of scripture and that preaching should be the sharing of God's word, not just the propounding of one's own ideas or thoughts.[25] When we are asked to give talks in sacrament meeting or help to plan our own sacrament services as part of a ward council, we may find this traditional model instructive. As we more fully incorporate God's word, found in both our written scriptures and the teachings of modern prophets and apostles, we can invoke the Spirit in a powerful way.

Because of widespread illiteracy in the Middle Ages, most people knew the scriptures only from hearing them read in Latin, a language few knew well, at church or by seeing biblical stories portrayed in stained glass windows or other church art. Even clergy were often only functionally literate, barely able to read the scriptural lessons. Many monastic communities, however, preserved the scriptures by lovingly copying them and regularly reading them. St. Benedict of Nursia (c. A.D. 480–547), who established a famous set of rules for western monasteries, was a proponent of *lectio divina*, or "divine reading." According to Benedict, this kind of reading was more than just reading through the text. Rather, it involved careful reading, meditating on each passage, praying about its meaning, and then contemplating, which meant taking the time to open one's heart and mind to listen to God. Reportedly, Benedict said, "You can read the book, or you can pray the book!"[26] Such a devotional approach to scripture makes reading more than a way to learn about God and his will for us. It is a way of actually encountering him, and as we read, intentionally and mindfully, his Spirit can change us, giving us a greater desire to love and serve God and the strength we need to do whatever his Spirit directs us to do.

The Qur'ān is the sacred text of Islam, being accepted as the word of God dictated to Muḥammad. Though it is the revelations in the Qur'ān and not the book itself that are holy, copies of the Qur'ān have long been treated with special reverence. Today, for instance, a family's copy of the Qur'ān may be kept in a special place on the highest shelf, wrapped in a special cover, and treated with great respect. The love of Muslims for the Qur'ān became particularly evident to me when my daughter, Rachel, and I visited the Ḥaram al-Sharīf, or Temple Mount, during the holy month of Ramaḍān. There we saw many worshippers, but the ones who impressed me most were a large number of women who sat together in a circle under a tree, studying and discussing their sacred scripture. As we have seen, devout Muslims will often read the entire Qur'ān during Ramaḍān, and memorizing the entire text is a special honor, giving a man the title *ḥāfiẓ* and a woman *ḥāfiẓa*.[27] Similarly, we treat copies of our scriptures reverently and memorize important passages that help us feel close to God, remind us of important truths, or inspire us.

As the sixteenth century opened and the Reformation approached, the worship of the medieval church focused almost exclusively on the liturgy of the Eucharist and had become less interactive for the congregation. The mass was said in Latin, a language most did not know, and in some places scriptural lessons had been replaced with stories from the lives of the saints, with little effective preaching. Martin Luther tried to change this pattern by insisting on the use of vernacular languages for ordinances and refocusing worship on the word of God, a move that was followed by other reformers. In the more conservative Protestant traditions, such as the Lutheran and Anglican, many of the older forms of worship were maintained, bolstered by reinvigorated scripture readings that were accompanied by preaching. Ulrich Zwingli (A.D. 1484–1531), a more radical Swiss reformer, eliminated almost all ritual, music, and other aids to worship so that services could focus on scripture alone. Among many groups, set readings from the scripture, which had been tied to the liturgical year, were eliminated, allowing the minister to select his own scriptural text as the focus of his preaching.[28] The translation of the Bible into vernacular languages and its widespread distribution after the invention of the printing press helped make studying God's word the focus of Protestant worship. Copies of the Bible could be found in many homes, allowing families to read and search the scriptures to see what God had to say to them. Even a poor family like the Smiths owned and read a family Bible, allowing Joseph not only to learn about God but to set out one spring morning to actually encounter him.

The Restoration and Scripture

I began my love affair with the scriptures when I was fourteen years old. That year we were studying the Old Testament in early-morning seminary. Our teacher expected it to be a chore to drag her class of teenagers through that difficult, long text. But as I read it, page after page, I was introduced to a new and exciting world. The peoples and kingdoms changed, but one character was constant—the Lord. In each year of my seminary experience, the next year's text was like the sequel in an exciting series. I learned to love the scriptures as a youth, with a special fondness for the New Testament.

When I was a freshman at Brigham Young University, I fell in love again with scripture. Susan Easton, my Book of Mormon teacher, shared with us how on average a different name or title for the Lord appeared every 1.7 verses. Eager to see what that frequency looked like, I bought a new, hardbound copy of the Book of Mormon and highlighted each title as I came upon it. I had gained a real testimony of the Book of Mormon in high school, mostly because I recognized the familiar voice of Jesus Christ as I read it. Now I was finding him again. That is how I learned that reading the scriptures, book after book, year after year, can be an ongoing journey of discovery and rediscovery.

The coming forth of the Book of Mormon was one of the pivotal, foundational events of the Restoration, one that strengthened our relationship with scripture. The Bible had long been important to other Christians, but differences in opinion when interpreting it had led to the formation of many different churches—ironically, much of this division occurred after the Reformation had focused believers on reading the Bible to find God's truth. One major purpose of the Book of Mormon, besides restoring plain and precious parts missing from the biblical record, was to "establish the truth" of the Bible (1 Nephi 13:40; see also vv. 34–36). This restoration occurs not only by the Book of Mormon's clarifying doctrines and beliefs that may be disputed in the Bible but also by confirming the Bible's importance and truthfulness at a time when modern scholarship has increasingly led some to question its veracity. A revelation underscored the importance of both volumes of scripture when the Lord called upon us to "remember the new covenant, even the Book of Mormon and the former commandments [the Bible] which I have given them, not only to say, but to do according to that which I have written" (D&C 84:57).

The coming forth of the Book of Mormon also opened the canon, preparing Latter-day Saints to accept still further scripture as the word of God. Accordingly, the early revelations of Joseph Smith were collected and published in 1833 as the Book of Commandments. When this collection was formally accepted by a general conference of the Church on August 17, 1835, the newly entitled Doctrine and Covenants became the third canonized book of scripture. Additional sections and official declarations have been added from time to time, most recently in 1981.[29] If the Bible had provided the foundation for Christianity, President Ezra Taft Benson, president of the Church from 1985 to 1994, taught that the Book of Mormon and the Doctrine and Covenants provide the keystone and the capstone of our religion.[30] Finally, we have the Pearl of Great Price, a collection of inspired documents that includes an extended excerpt from Joseph Smith's inspired revision of Genesis (the book of Moses); a revealed portion of writings from Abraham; Joseph Smith's revision of Matthew 23:39–24:51 (Joseph Smith–Matthew); and an extract from Joseph Smith's history, including the 1838 account of his First Vision (Joseph Smith–History). Modern revelation further makes clear that scripture includes inspired teaching and preaching, especially by our sustained leaders (D&C 68:4).

Moroni's promise, which assures us that we will know by the power of the Holy Ghost that the Book of Mormon is true if we read, ponder, and ask God in faith (Moroni 10:3–5), is a promise that we can apply to *all* scripture—to the word of the Lord whenever it was written and wherever we find it. Carefully and prayerfully reading the scriptures, pondering them, and waiting for inspiration to come to us can be powerful ways of worshipping. This is not only a worship of the mind but also of the heart, because as we learn about God, Christ, and the gospel, we are filled with love for them. As we are mindful of the Spirit moving within us, guiding us, and empowering us, we set forth from scripture study to better live the gospel and serve the Lord with all our strength. Accepting these words and letting them swell and grow in our hearts builds faith as they bring us to Jesus Christ, who is a tree springing up to everlasting life (Alma 32:32–33, 40–41).

To use the word of the Lord—written, read, spoken, and preached—more effectively as a form of worship, we need to use it more deliberately, more often, and with more awareness of what it is and what potential power it carries. Reading, whether aloud to a group or silently to ourselves, can become perfunctory, even rote. Thus, intentionality—realizing what we are doing and being able to actually conceive that we are receiving God's word from him—is vital. Just as our Jewish friends have taught that prayer is just words without *kavanah,* without reverence for scripture and faith in it, reading may not always be an experience of worship. In private study, I have found it helps to have a regular set time and place to read the scriptures. In that sense, we can create a sacred space—not only temporally and spatially but also mentally and spiritually—to be with the Lord.

Reading the scriptures often begins as a way of worshipping the Lord with our minds by studying the words and drawing lessons and principles from them. Often academic references and other resources can help provide historical, cultural, and linguistic background. Elder David A. Bednar has further encouraged us to study the scriptures carefully by cross-referencing, exploring topics, and finding patterns and connections so that we can apply the scriptures to ourselves.[31] In addition, immersing ourselves in the word can also be a way of worshipping the Lord with our hearts as we seek to have scripture bring the Spirit into our worship. The medieval practice of *lectio divina,* or "divine reading," is as much about the feelings and experiences we have when we read as it is what we learn. This approach encourages us to read slowly and deliberately, perhaps aloud, rather than reading a set number of pages or chapters or for a fixed amount of time. Such devotional reading encourages us to stop to reflect on passages as we read, considering how they apply to us, opening our hearts to the Lord, asking questions, and expressing praise.

Finally, as with intense prayer, engaging with the scriptures can be as much about listening as it is about reading, leading us to pause during and sit quietly afterwards to wait upon the Lord. Such mindfulness allows scripture study to become a catalyst for worshipping with our strength: we finish our feast renewed, changed, and inspired to act. Reading and studying the scriptures then brings power into our lives, including the ability to hear the Lord's voice (D&C 18:35–36), teach and exhort each other (D&C 25:7; 97:3–5), answer questions (Alma

12:1; 21:9), liken the scriptures to ourselves (1 Nephi 19:23), and press forward in Christ as we endure to the end (2 Nephi 31:20; 32:3).[32]

In addition to being a bigger part of our personal worship, using the scriptures more frequently in our sacrament meetings and church classes will help those experiences be more worshipful.[33] As ward councils, we can suggest to the bishopric meeting themes that are based on scriptural passages rather than just topics for our talks. As speakers and teachers, we can integrate the scriptures and the words of the living prophets more fully into our talks and lessons. Sometimes changing the way we speak about our church meetings can affect the way we think about them: referring to sacrament meeting as a sacrament *service* emphasizes the ordinance we have gathered to celebrate, and asking ward members to *teach* a topic or *preach* the gospel focuses us on principles and the word of the Lord more than does asking them simply to give a talk—we are, after all, enjoined to teach and preach the gospel, not to get together just to talk about it![34] Elder M. Russell Ballard, one of the Twelve since 1985, taught, "Those who are entrusted to speak and teach in our meetings need to do so with doctrinal power that will be both heard and felt, lifting the spirits and edifying our people. . . . The Spirit cannot be restrained when pure testimony of Christ is borne."[35] One of the best ways to set the stage for such pure testimony is to use the scriptures more.

Holidays and other important days, particularly Christmas and Easter, are sacred times that provide important opportunities to highlight the scriptures and, as we shall see, use music as a form of worship. While extended scripture readings are not the usual or expected pattern in our sacrament meetings, holidays are ideal times to use scriptural narratives to tell the stories of Jesus' birth, Passion, and resurrection. They can also be used to commemorate such other occasions as the restoration of the priesthood or events from biblical or Church history with a power that is uniquely theirs.

Scripture can be particularly powerful at a funeral. At our mother's funeral, my sister gave the life sketch, we had two short tributes, beautiful music, and a concluding sermon by me. However, one of the most moving features of her memorial service was the frequent reading of scripture. Between the talks and musical numbers, we divided the six grandchildren into pairs and had them read passages that fit the occasion. My nieces, nephews, and children read psalms of praise for God's goodness and psalms that alluded to the temple (Psalms 23:1–24:5; 150); the passage from the Doctrine and Covenants about music, which Mom loved so much (D&C 25:12–13); the story of how Jesus comforted Martha and Mary at Lazarus's death (John 11:21–27, 32–33, 35); and finally a beautiful passage describing the heavenly Jerusalem and how there would be no more sorrow or tears there (Revelation 21:1–4). These passages brought the Spirit to the funeral in a powerful way and taught doctrine more directly than any of us could.

Elder Robert D. Hales, a member of the Council of the Twelve Apostles since 1994, said the following about the purpose of scriptures and how they can constitute real, powerful encounters with God:

"When we want to speak to God, we pray. And when we want Him to speak to us, we search the scriptures; for His words are spoken through His prophets. He will then teach us as we listen to the promptings of the Holy Spirit.

"If you have not heard His voice speaking to you lately, return with new eyes and new ears to the scriptures."[36]

The word of God—read, preached, and taught—is indeed the voice of God to us. It engenders reverence, quickens the mind, changes hearts, and inspires action. As we prepare ourselves to receive it, focus upon it, and accept its direction, it is a vital way of worshipping the Lord.

6

WORSHIPPING GOD THROUGH MUSIC

The Song of the Righteous Is a Prayer unto the Lord

> *Make a joyful noise unto the Lord, all the earth:*
> *make a loud noise, and rejoice, and sing praise.*
> *Sing unto the Lord with the harp;*
> *with the harp, and the voice of a psalm.*
> *With trumpets and sound of cornet*
> *make a joyful noise before the Lord, the King.*
> —Psalm 98:4–6
>
> *For my soul delighteth in the song of the heart;*
> *yea, the song of the righteous is a prayer unto me,*
> *and it shall be answered with a blessing upon their heads.*
> —Doctrine & Covenants 25:12

Music is found in every culture and is a basic feature of human life. It has a profound ability both to express and to impress. Through it we can express a full range of our feelings and desires, often better than we can through words alone. It also has a powerful ability to influence how we feel, think, and act. As a result, it can be a particularly potent means of worship. Craig Jessop, director of the Mormon Tabernacle Choir from 1999 to 2008 and dean of the Caine College of the Arts at Utah State University since 2010, explained, "Music is the first art . . . and vocal music is the first of the firsts. It is the basic yearning of the human spirit to express love, thanks, devotion, and praise to God."[1] If prayer is the soul's sincere desire, then music is the heart's most earnest expression.

But for music to be more than a way of expressing ourselves or being influenced, for it to truly be a means of worship, we cannot simply sing, play, or listen to it. We must deliberately intend it to be worship, which requires that we perform it or enjoy it with the awareness that it is meant to praise God and draw us closer to him. Verena Ursenbach Hatch (1922–2012), a Latter-day Saint musician and author, observed that when properly experienced, music can be worship: "First as an act of worship, it provides the vehicle or medium by which man actually communes with God through song. Second, as an aid to worship, it prepares an emotional climate in which worship can take place."[2]

As we seek to use music as a form of worship, how does it prepare us for other ways of approaching God? How was it used in the scriptures and through history to create such wonderful space for worship, particularly before prayer or ordinances? What must we do to make hymn singing praise and not just a routine part of our meetings? When we share a musical number, how can we make it an offering rather than a performance? As we listen to beautiful music, how can we more spiritually engage with it? How does it change us for the better?

Music in Ancient Israel

While in New York City with the Mormon Tabernacle Choir during the summer of 2015, my friend Andy and I attended a morning service at St. Bartholomew's Episcopal Church in Manhattan. Because we were there during the church's summer music festival, the service featured a small, fine choir and instrumentalists who performed movements from Leonard Bernstein's *Chichester Psalms*. A striking work composed for the Southern Cathedrals Festival at Chichester, England, in 1965, *Chichester Psalms* is noteworthy for presenting several of the Psalms in their original Hebrew. Employing a harp, timpani, unusual harmonies, and haunting melodies, its musical scoring is intended to be reminiscent of ancient Jewish music.

I have sung the *Chichester Psalms* on two occasions with the Tabernacle Choir, but as Andy and I listened to it in the context of an Anglican worship service complete with a high altar, prayers, and liberal use of incense, I was transported back to what musical worship of the Lord must have been like in the ancient temple at Jerusalem.

Although music probably began with Adam and Eve and their family, the earliest biblical reference to music or musical instruments is Genesis 4:21, where as part of the general rise of human civilization, Jubal invented stringed instruments, probably the lyre, and the pipe (KJV, "harp and organ"). The first recorded reference to singing, particularly singing a song of praise, occurs after the crossing of the Red Sea when Moses and then Miriam and the women of Israel sing praises to the Lord for his victory over Pharaoh's army and their deliverance from bondage (Exodus 15:1–21). Although we do not know anything about the melodies or type of music used by the children of Israel, the text that has been preserved is poetic, employing parallelism like the later psalms and manifesting an ability to stir emotion. At the conclusion of his ministry, Moses sang another song to Israel, which served as a musical and poetic reminder of the Lord's goodness to them and the dangers of apostasy and unfaithfulness (Deuteronomy 31:30–32:44).[3]

During the reign of the judges, Deborah and Barak sang an inspired song of victory after the Lord had delivered Israel from Sisera and the Canaanites (Judges 5). Later a band of prophets is described as worshipping with lyre, tambourine, pipe, and harp (1 Samuel 10:5; KJV, a "psaltery" and a "tabret"). Perhaps one of the most beautiful early songs in the Old Testament is the Song of Hannah, which poetically represents her prayer of thanksgiving and praise at the time she dedicated her first son, Samuel, to the Lord:

> *My heart rejoiceth in the Lord, mine horn is exalted in the Lord:*
> > *my mouth is enlarged over mine enemies;*
> > *because I rejoice in thy salvation.*
>
> *There is none holy as the Lord:*
> > *for there is none beside thee:*
> > *neither is there any rock like our God. . . .*
>
> *The Lord killeth, and maketh alive:*
> > *he bringeth down to the grave, and bringeth up.*

WORSHIPPING GOD THROUGH MUSIC

> *The Lord maketh poor, and maketh rich:*
>   *he bringeth low, and lifteth up. . . .*
> *The Lord shall judge the ends of the earth;*
>   *and he shall give strength unto his king,*
>   *and exalt the horn of his anointed. (1 Samuel 2:1–10)*

With David we first have significant information about how music was used in the worship of the Lord in Old Testament times. Described as a skilled lyre player and singer, David soothed the troubled king Saul and drove away evil spirits with the power of his music (1 Samuel 16:14–23; 18:10). Similarly, President Boyd K. Packer taught about the power of good music over evil thoughts and influences in our lives.[4]

David was also a gifted poet and composer of psalms who acknowledged that his words were inspired by the Spirit of God. He is credited with having been the first to organize music for formal worship. First, David arranged for Levites to sing and play instruments to welcome the ark of the covenant when he brought it to Jerusalem (1 Chronicles 15:16). Then, in preparation for the temple that Solomon would build, David carefully organized twenty-four groups of musicians to minister before the altar musically, using instruments and singing to praise the Lord (1 Chronicles 6:16–48; 23; 25). Biblical scholar Daniel Block observed, "In David we witness the rare combination of deep spirituality, extraordinary musical giftedness, and exceptional organizational acumen,"[5] traits that we have seen in some of the great composers and choir and orchestra directors of our day.

Although not all the psalms attributed to David were necessarily composed by him, his early compositions inspired what became one of Israel's greatest poetic and musical forms, the psalms. Poetry, as concentrated, creative, and evocative use of language, has a great potential to stir both emotional and spiritual feelings. In Hebrew, the poetic effects of the psalms are accomplished largely through parallelism, a technique by which a phrase is followed by a second phrase that either restates the first, contrasts with it, or builds upon it. The effect is to focus the attention of the hearer or reader on the meaning. Psalms are "songs of praise" (Hebrew, *tehillîm;* Greek, *psalmoi*) that include a wide range of feelings expressed to God, ranging from complaint, praise, and thanksgiving to celebrations of the king as the anointed representative of the Lord and the Torah as his word. Many of them had a liturgical function describing the joys of worshipping the Lord in his house and celebrating his kingship and greatness.[6] As noted by biblical scholar Barry Bandstra, if Torah was the revelation of God's will and prophecy was its proclamation, then the psalms reflect the response of worshippers to their encounters with God.[7] Because the psalms capture so well the feelings we often have toward God or want to share with him, reading them even today can help us feel close to the Lord.

The inherent meaning of the psalms and the power of their poetry were augmented by their musical performance. Anciently the psalms were sung and were often accompanied by instruments.[8] That musical accompaniment was particularly important in the temple, where following David's pattern of performing the psalms was an important part of the worship.[9] An example is seen during the reign of King Hezekiah, who "set the Levites in the house of the Lord with cymbals, with psalteries, and with harps, according to the commandment of David. . . . And the Levites stood with the instruments of David, and the priests with the trumpets. And Hezekiah commanded to offer the burnt offering upon the altar. And *when the burnt offering began, the song of the Lord began also with the trumpets, and with the instruments ordained by David king of Israel.* And all the congregation worshipped, and the singers sang, and the trumpeters sounded" (2 Chronicles 29:25–28; emphasis added).

This pattern suggests that ancient temple worship was a dynamic, awe-inspiring experience, involving all the senses—the sight of sacrifices and ritual gestures, the smell of burnt offerings and incense, and the sound of prayers and music sung by groups of singers and multiple instrument players.[10] Nevertheless, in a very broad sense, ancient religious music parallels our own practice, with prelude and postlude music framing our sacrament meetings, hymns preceding our prayers, and the sacrament hymn preparing us for the administration of the sacrament itself. Perhaps we could very loosely compare the Levitical temple choir and players to our Mormon Tabernacle Choir and Orchestra at Temple Square, each adding to our worship and deepening it with their music.

Music in the New Testament

At the end of my freshman year at Brigham Young University, I had the opportunity to sing Robert Cundick's *Redeemer* with the BYU combined choirs. Brother Cundick, Tabernacle organist from 1965 to 1991, composed *The Redeemer* at the request of Ralph Woodward, music professor at Brigham Young University, who had selected scriptures from all four Latter-day Saint standard works for "a musical service depicting the doctrines and Atonement of Jesus Christ." The combination of scriptural testimony and stirring musical settings produced a Restoration oratorio that spans the prophesied coming of the Redeemer, the achievement of his atoning sacrifice, and the promise that it offers us.[11]

As a freshman, I had an earnest but young testimony of the gospel of Jesus Christ. I certainly had come to love the Savior, but singing such beautiful music about his mission touched my heart and soul in totally new ways. I felt spiritual affirmation that I had not experienced before and was filled with assurance that Jesus was God's only Son, who came to earth to suffer, die, and rise for me. That experience reaffirmed something that I had learned much earlier from my mother: music is a powerful way to gain, deepen, and share testimony.

The first musical expressions in the New Testament appear in the nativity stories of Luke. Known in church tradition and scholarship as canticles ("songs"), in their final form these are poetic renditions in Greek that movingly express the sentiments of such characters as Mary when she visited Elisabeth (the *Magnificat,* Luke 1:46–55), Zacharias at the blessing of John the Baptist (the *Benedictus,* Luke 1:68–79), the angels outside of Bethlehem (the *Gloria in excelsis,* Luke 2:14), and Simeon in the temple (the *Nunc dimittis,* Luke 2:29–32). For us as modern readers, they personalize the characters even as they draw us into the story, encouraging us to compare our situation to theirs and see how the Lord is similarly moving in our lives.[12] These canticles were beloved of early Christians, serving in a sense as the earliest Christmas carols because of their association with Jesus' birth. In the Middle Ages they were set to music and incorporated into many religious services. The *Magnificat,* for instance, is often sung or read in morning prayer services, helping worshippers reflect on how they, like Mary of old, can magnify the Lord by bringing Jesus into the world that day. Similarly, the *Nunc dimittis,* in which Simeon declared that he could now die in peace because he had at last seen the Lord, is often used in evening services as an ending to the day.

The next direct reference to music during the ministry of Jesus occurs at the end of the Last Supper, where Mark, followed by Matthew, relates that Jesus and his disciples "had sung an hymn" before they went to Gethsemane (Mark 14:26; parallel Matthew 26:30). This was likely one of the so-called Hallel Psalms (Psalms 113–18), which are traditionally sung at joyful holidays, especially Passover. The focus of these psalms in blessing the Lord, trusting in him, and crying for salvation fit the occasion, both of Passover generally and of Jesus' Passion in particular.[13] Particularly poignant, given what Jesus was about to go through, is the following:

> *The sorrows of death compassed me,*
>   *and the pains of hell gat hold upon me:*
>   *I found trouble and sorrow.*
> *Then called I upon the name of the Lord;*
>   *O Lord, I beseech thee, deliver my soul. (Psalm 116:3–4)*

Acts 16:25 refers to Paul and Silas praying and singing praises to God all night while they were in the prison at Philippi, and the letters of Paul make several references to singing as a form of worship. While discussing correct forms of worship with the Corinthians, Paul described his own way of worshipping:

> *I will pray with the spirit,*
>   *and I will pray with the understanding also:*
> *I will sing with the spirit,*
>   *and I will sing with the understanding also. (1 Corinthians 14:15; emphasis added)*

Though the original context compares praying and singing with full understanding to the ecstatic worship of the Corinthians in unknown tongues, the emphasis of doing both "with the spirit" continues to be important today. Prayer and singing are seen as parallel forms of worship when they are done with the Spirit, which gives meaning and understanding to both of these acts of worship. Colossians and Ephesians provide closely parallel exhortations to use singing as a means of experiencing the Spirit, edifying one another, expressing gratitude, and glorifying God by "singing and making melody in your heart" (Ephesians 5:19; see Colossians 3:16–17; Ephesians 5:18–20).

Perhaps more significant than passages about sacred music are fragments of early Christian hymns that appear in the writings attributed to Paul. If these are early Hebrew or Aramaic songs that Paul has translated for his readers' use, they may represent some of the earliest Christian hymns.[14] Because they almost all have to do with Jesus Christ and his role as Creator and Redeemer, they are usually called Christological hymns. A beautiful example is found in Paul's letter to the Philippians, which breaks into two stanzas, one describing Jesus' condescension and the other his exaltation:

> *Let this mind be in you, which was also in Christ Jesus:*
>
> *Who, being in the form of God,*
> *thought it not robbery to be equal with God:*
> *But made himself of no reputation,*
> *and took upon him the form of a servant,*
> *and was made in the likeness of men:*
> *And being found in fashion as a man,*
> *he humbled himself,*
> *and became obedient unto death, even the death of the cross.*
>
> *Wherefore God also hath highly exalted him,*
> *and given him a name which is above every name:*
> *That at the name of Jesus every knee should bow,*
> *of things in heaven, and things in earth,*
> *and things under the earth;*

> *And that every tongue should confess*
> *that Jesus Christ is Lord,*
> *to the glory of God the Father. (Philippians 2:5–11)*

The final New Testament references to music are the songs and hymn fragments that appear in the book of Revelation, which John presents as being sung by heavenly figures at different points in the world's history.[15] Some allude to Old Testament models or have parallels with them, but many are unique compositions, revealing how worship takes place in heaven. This heavenly worship depicts the heavenly hosts bowing down before God, offering prayers, and singing, all focusing on Jesus as the Lamb of God and his saving work.[16] For instance, when the Lamb of God takes the sealed scroll, four beasts and twenty-four elders fall down before him, play harps, and sing. Afterward, they are joined by tens of thousands of angels who sing,

> *Worthy is the Lamb that was slain*
> *to receive power, and riches, and wisdom,*
> *and strength, and honour, and glory, and blessing. (Revelation 5:12)*

Every creature above, on, and under the earth then joins in one resounding hymn of praise, singing

> *Blessing, and honour, and glory, and power,*
> *be unto him that sitteth upon the throne,*
> *and unto the Lamb for ever and ever. (Revelation 5:13)*

This and several of the other songs are familiar to modern audiences because of the efforts of George Frideric Handel, who included portions of them in some of the great choruses of his oratorio *Messiah*. The lyrics are stirring precisely because they represent the most divine type of worship. Though none of the melodies of New Testament songs survive, they underscore the importance of music in praising and drawing near to God.

WORSHIPPING GOD THROUGH MUSIC

A Brief Overview of the Development of Religious Music

In the summer of 2009, I spent two weeks in England as part of an academic fellowship. At the end of one beautiful day in Cambridge, I entered King's College right before the celebration of evensong, the daily service of musical prayer that has been held almost every day for centuries. Because there were few people in attendance, I was able to sit in the north choir stalls, directly across from the choristers who would sing the service.

As the marvelous organ played the introit, the minister, the choristers, and their director processed in. I was carried away in time, realizing that this form of worship went back to some of the earliest days of Christianity in England. Psalms were sung antiphonally, with one part of the choir singing in response to the other. Lessons from the Old and New Testament were read, after which the choir sang in Latin the *Magnificat,* Mary's wonderful song of praise from Luke 1:46-55, and the *Nunc dimittis,* the inspired words of Simeon when he saw the baby Jesus in the temple. After further prayers and a short homily, or sermon, the choir sang a beautiful anthem accompanied by the organ. Holy space, sacred time, prayer, and above all music combined in that hour in a wonderful celebration of worshipful praise.

With the destruction of the temple in Jerusalem, Jewish worship through music as it had been known came to an end. Instrumental music has been banned from traditional synagogues as an ongoing sign of mourning ever since, but the Jewish tradition still recognizes the power of music to stir the soul and bring it closer to God. Poetic portions of scripture had long been sung or chanted, and such chanting continues to give Hebrew scripture a spiritual quality that can powerfully move listeners.[17]

Vocal music also came to serve an important role in prayer in the synagogue. Rabbi Judah he-Ḥasid (c. 1150–1217) wrote, "Say your prayers in a melody that is most pleasant and sweet to you. Then you shall pray with proper *kavanah,* because the melody will draw your heart after the words that come from your mouth."[18] Accordingly, synagogue services developed beautiful musical prayers called the *nûsaḥ.* These musical prayers are usually sung by a specially trained singer called a *ḥazzān,* or cantor. He is known as the "emissary of the congregation" because the melody of his singing carries their prayers to heaven.[19] Music similarly became a vital part of home worship in Jewish families, particularly in the form of traditional songs called *zemîrôt,* which are regularly sung as part of the Sabbath meal.[20]

Augustine of Hippo (354–430) is often credited with having said, "He who sings prays twice," suggesting that the Christian singer serves much the same role as the Jewish cantor, conveying prayer to God through the medium of music.[21] Early Christians borrowed much from early Jewish temple music, particularly the antiphonal, or responsorial, singing of psalms. In antiphonal singing, the leader of a congregation chants the first verse of a psalm and the congregation responds with the parallel verse that follows. After Christianity became a legal religion in the fourth century, new church music developed rapidly. In this period of musical productivity, Ambrose of Milan (c. 340–397) became known as the father of hymnody in the Western church because of the number of hymns he composed. The texts of some, such as *Veni redemptor gentium* ("Come, Redeemer of the Nations"), have survived, but because of a lack of musical notation, the melodies are unknown.

Plainsong, also known as Gregorian chant, developed in the ninth and tenth centuries in Western Europe. Sung in unison with the musical line shaped by its words, plainsong is hauntingly beautiful and stirs deep, reflective, spiritual feelings. Gregorian chant was particularly well-suited to monastic communities, which were united in worship by singing together. One of the drawbacks of music in the medieval period, however, was that the congregation participated less and singing became the prerogative of the clergy and religious orders. Religious architecture reflected this division: the congregation watched and listened from the nave while the clergy and monks sat and sang in the choir, which was the area that extended from the nave to the apse, where the altar was. Music in the late Middle Ages changed with the rediscovery of polyphony, which is the singing of many voice parts at the same time. This period also saw the gradual introduction of the pipe organ into cathedrals and other large churches. The more complex vocal music together with the reintroduction of instruments set the stage for later Christian music.[22]

In the Islamic tradition, the Qurʾān says nothing explicit about music, and the traditions of Muḥammad's opinion about it are somewhat mixed. Generally, the "art of sound" (Arabic, *handasah al ṣawt*) is neutral, but there is a recognition that the wrong kind of music can be distracting and even dangerous if it leads people away from God. Chanting the Qurʾān, however, like Jewish chanting of the Hebrew scripture and Christian responsive psalm singing, can be a powerful way of turning people to God. The most pervasive religious musical form in Islam is the *adhān,* the five-times daily call to prayer.[23] Although recorded prayer calls are sometimes used today, traditionally each mosque has a muezzin, a man able to cry out the prayer call loudly, melodiously, and beautifully. The power of a beautifully executed *adhān* can stir the irreligious, and even a non-Muslim can feel its pull. During my time in the Middle East, the sound of the prayer call regularly made me think about God and offer my own silent prayer in response to hearing the *adhān*.

The Reformation brought about renewed interest in Christian religious music. Martin Luther loved music, and one of his greatest contributions was the reintroduction of congregational singing. No longer the preserve of monastic or professional choirs, singing became a central part of worship for the entire congregation. Luther was the composer of at least thirty-seven hymns, including "A Mighty Fortress Is Our God," which appears in our own hymnbook. "Characterized by 'a plain melody, a strong harmony and a stately rhythm,'"[24] his hymns have the potential to stir powerful feelings about God and create a desire to worship and serve him. Luther also approved of instrumental music, preparing the way for Johann Sebastian Bach (1685–1750), who composed organ preludes and toccatas as well as chorales, cantatas, oratorios, and passions for church performances. During his time as music director of St. Thomas Church in Leipzig, Bach composed a cantata for each Sunday and every additional religious holiday of the year.[25]

Other reformers did not share Luther's openness to instrumental music, largely because the New Testament never mentions it. Ulrich Zwingli (1484–1531), a leader of the Reformation in Switzerland, removed the organs from churches in Zurich and even forbade singing for a time. Other groups, such as the Calvinists and the Puritans, approved only the singing of psalms. But in England developments in religious music continued, and we are beneficiaries of that rich tradition. Isaac Watts (1674–1748), for instance, published a collection of English paraphrases of Psalms in 1719 that were more conducive to singing. His purpose in producing such paraphrases was to produce more pleasing texts that would not only help singers understand what they were singing but also be moved more deeply by the lyrics.[26] Watts composed many new hymns, several of which are in the current Latter-day Saint hymnbook, including "Come, We That Love the Lord," the sacrament hymn "He Died! The Great Redeemer Died," and the Christmas carol "Joy to the World."[27] Other great hymn composers were John and Charles Wesley, leaders of the Methodist movement.[28] They felt that hymns served not only to praise the Lord but also to teach doctrine, leading Charles to compose more than six thousand hymns, including "Rejoice, the Lord Is King!" and "Christ the Lord Is Risen Today," both of which appear in our hymnbook.[29] England was also the second home of Handel (1685–1759), who composed *Messiah* as an enduring musical testimony of Jesus Christ and his mission.

Roman Catholic services tended to involve congregations less than Protestant ones did, but religious music flourished in that tradition as well, often producing dramatic settings of the mass that could make services virtual concerts. Giovanni Pierluigi da Palestrina (c. 1525–1594), for example, excelled at writing sophisticated music in which beautiful polyphony accented but did not overwhelm the text of the service that was being sung.[30] Palestrina influenced subsequent composers, both Catholic and Protestant; Palestrina's masses were an important inspiration for Bach, for instance.[31] Later religious pieces, including the masses and requiems of such great composers as Wolfgang Amadeus Mozart, were numbered alongside their secular works, but the nonreligious works of Bach, Handel, and Mozart reveal the spiritual potential of great music even when it is not directly used in worship. Art, including and especially music, can be an important mediator between nature and God, who created the world in an orderly and beautiful way. In Bach's time, harmony symbolized the order of nature and its divine cause, so in well-composed and stirring music "God is honored and praised but mankind is moved to devotion, virtue, joy, and sorrow."[32]

Music in the Restoration

During the afternoon session of general conference on Sunday, October 1, 2006, two of the hymns that I sang with the Mormon Tabernacle Choir touched me deeply, being instances of true musical worship. The first was Mack Wilberg's stirring arrangement of the familiar Thanksgiving hymn "Come, Ye Thankful People, Come," by Henry Alford.[33] After the familiar first two verses, we sang the following additional verses, which sing of the Second Coming and how Christ will take us back to live in his presence:

For the Lord our God shall come,
And shall take His harvest home;
From His field shall in that day
All offenses purge away,
Giving angels charge at last
In the fire the tares to cast;
But the fruitful ears to store
In His garner evermore.

Even so, Lord, quickly come
To Thy final Harvest Home;
Gather Thou Thy people in,
Free from sorrow, free from sin,
There, forever purified,

> *In Thy presence to abide;*
> *Come, with all Thine angels, come,*
> *Raise the glorious harvest home.*[34]

The closing hymn was the beloved Latter-day Saint hymn "We Thank Thee, O God, for a Prophet." President Gordon B. Hinckley had had surgery for intestinal cancer earlier that year, and in his closing remarks he testified of his remarkable recovery and thanked the Lord for His goodness. As we sang, we felt gratitude for a latter-day prophet. As Brother Jessop turned and had the audience join us for the final verse, one by one people throughout the Conference Center began to stand. We were incredibly moved, feeling the Lord's love for his servant. I was overcome with emotion and could not keep singing. Few of my fellow Choir members were able to keep singing either. Nevertheless, the loft was filled with powerful, angelic music, and I knew that we were not alone in singing of God's goodness and mercy that day.

Frontier settlers like the Smith family would have had little exposure to such musical greats as Bach, Handel, and Mozart. But in addition to secular folk music, the Smiths would have been very familiar with frontier congregational singing. The kind of folk musical traditions that were common in the Methodist and Baptist camp meetings attended by the young Joseph Smith can be found in such collections as *Southern Harmony* (1835) and *Sacred Harp* (1844).[35] Joseph's family was musical. His father, Joseph Smith Sr., had been a music teacher and led his family in singing hymns each evening. Hymn singing had been part of Lucy Mack Smith's musical upbringing as well, and she might have been a member of the Palmyra Presbyterian choir when she and three of her children joined that church.[36] The Smith family's experience would have been similar to that of many of the first Latter-day Saints: some would have come from a background of singing folk hymns at camp meetings, some would been familiar with the more formal hymns and choir singing of established Protestant churches, and many would have been exposed to both.

Emma Hale, who married Joseph Smith in 1827, came from a Methodist family in Harmony, Pennsylvania, so she would have been familiar with Methodist patterns of hymn singing. In July 1830 Emma received a revelation through Joseph that called upon her "to make a selection of sacred hymns, as it shall be given thee, which is pleasing unto me, to be had in my church. For my soul delighteth in the song of the heart; yea, the song of the righteous is a prayer unto me, and it shall be answered with a blessing upon their heads" (D&C 25:11–12). This direction was preceded by a mandate for her to expound the scriptures and devote herself to writing and learning, all of which were useful to her in selecting hymns that would help the Saints praise God and learn his truths. Michael Hicks, a music professor at Brigham Young University, has noted that because the selection had to come from the repertoire of other churches, the revelation acknowledged the inherent merit of those musical traditions. Furthermore, "it equated sacred singing with praying, making vocal music, in effect, requisite to worship."[37]

Emma's collection became the basis for the Church's first hymnbook, which was published in 1836. Entitled *A Collection of Sacred Hymns for the Church of the Latter Day Saints,* this 127-page hymnal contained only the hymn texts, which worshippers would then sing to familiar tunes. About fifty of the hymns had Protestant origins; another forty were by Latter-day Saints, particularly W. W. Phelps. John Tullidge compiled and published *Latter Day Saints' Psalmody* in 1857, and in January 1884 the *Deseret Sunday School Union Music Book* was issued. Both of these were compiled and published in Utah Territory and included music as well as texts, much of which was newly composed by Latter-day Saints. President Heber J. Grant, president of the Church from 1918 to 1945, formed the Church Music Committee in 1920, which, after years of work, produced *Latter-day Saints Hymns* in 1927.[38]

All of these hymnbooks and their successors have provided members of the Church the means to worship through song as they have gathered together in sacrament services, Sunday School, meetings of auxiliaries, and families. The most recent official collection, *Hymns of The Church of Jesus Christ of Latter-day Saints,* was published in 1985. This collection of sacred songs begins with inspired direction from the

First Presidency in its preface that explains how these hymns should be used in our church meetings, homes, and personal lives:

"Inspirational music is an essential part of our church meetings. The hymns invite the Spirit of the Lord, create a feeling of reverence, unify us as members, and provide a way for us to offer praises to the Lord.

"Some of the greatest sermons are preached by the singing of hymns. Hymns move us to repentance and good works, build testimony and faith, comfort the weary, console the mourning, and inspire us to endure to the end."[39]

This instruction presents sacred music as having the essential features of worship. First, it invites the Spirit of the Lord, which produces worship of the heart, exhibited by reverence. It also cultivates the worship of the mind as we praise the Lord and learn about him through "sermons preached by the singing of the hymns." Further, inspirational music results in worshipping the Lord with our strength as it changes us and enables us to do his will through repentance, good works, charity, and enduring to the end.

Music shapes our communal worship, but we must be mindful and make deliberate effort for it to influence us spiritually. Prelude and postlude music frame our worship services, helping us prepare to worship by effectively demarcating sacred time. The prelude invites the Spirit and helps us prepare for the prayers, preaching, and ordinances that follow, but a lovely musical introduction and the postlude that follows the meeting are nothing but background noise if we chat, rush in late, surf on our cell phones, or let other matters preoccupy us while they are being played. The opening and closing hymns are closely connected to the invocation and benediction that they precede, but they become prayers themselves if we realize that we are actually singing to God. Sacrament hymns are particularly sacred, providing us an opportunity to testify how Jesus suffered and died for us before we participate in the ordinance of the Lord's Supper. Regardless of musical ability, each of us is encouraged by the First Presidency to worship by singing the hymns, and if we do so by concentrating and setting aside outside influences and concerns, we can encounter the Lord in a powerful way.

Hymn singing is not the only music that requires our participation to be effective as worship; listening to the ward choir sing or the performance of a special musical number performed requires mindful, spiritual attention as well. To ensure that the influence of music will be felt appropriately, bishoprics in wards and presiding authorities in other gatherings are responsible to see that musical texts and styles of singing and playing are appropriate for the type of meeting being held. Ward, branch, and stake choirs play an important part in our communal worship by inviting the Spirit through hymns, hymn arrangements, or other appropriate religious music. An earnest choir that seeks the Spirit can have much the same effect in a ward meeting that the Mormon Tabernacle Choir has in general conferences of the Church.

The Mormon Tabernacle Choir has played a significant role in Latter-day Saint worship for much of its history. The Choir has its roots in a large group of Welsh singers who entered the Salt Lake Valley in 1849 and attracted the attention of Brigham Young. They became the nucleus of the choir that was formed for the dedication of the Salt Lake Tabernacle on April 6, 1852. From the beginning, the choir sang not only hymns but also great choral masterworks, such as those of Handel, Franz Josef Haydn, and Felix Mendelssohn. Though the Tabernacle's famous organ has been the Choir's usual accompaniment and serves a worship and performing role all its own, the Choir had full orchestral accompaniment in performances as early as 1855. It was officially joined by the Orchestra at Temple Square in 1998, recreating the same kind of partnership between vocal and instrumental music that had existed in the ancient temple in Jerusalem. A long chain of conductors, assistants, organists, and singers have helped the Tabernacle Choir develop its signature sound, each generation standing on the shoulders of those who have gone before. In addition to singing for Church conferences and events, the Choir and Orchestra fulfill their musical mission through weekly broadcasts of *Music and the Spoken Word,* which began in 1929, as well as through concerts, tours, and recordings for wide audiences within and outside of the Church.[40]

Whether heard or sung, religious songs, particularly the hymns, have a great potential to teach. One of the last priesthood training broadcasts that I attended as a bishop years ago featured President Boyd K. Packer, who, pointing to three bound volumes, said, "In these books are the doctrine of the Church." The volumes were the Bible, the triple combination of the Book of Mormon, the Doctrine and Covenants, and the Pearl of Great Price, and the hymnbook.[41] Our hymns have been carefully selected to ensure not only doctrinal reliability but inspiration. Beginning with songs of the Restoration, the hymnbook proceeds with songs of praise, gratitude, and comfort and continues with sacrament, Christmas, and Easter hymns. The latter part of the book has a variety of songs of encouragement, instruction, home, and loyalty. All of these include cross-references with scriptures that allow them to be part of family and personal study as well as for church use. In regard to using the hymns in the home, the preface teaches:

"Music has boundless powers for moving families toward greater spirituality and devotion to the gospel. Latter-day Saints should fill their homes with the sound of worthy music.

"Ours is a hymnbook for the home as well as for the meetinghouse. We hope the hymnbook will take a prominent place among the scriptures and other religious books in our homes. The hymns can bring families a spirit of beauty and peace and can inspire love and unity among family members."[42]

The hymnbook and the *Children's Songbook* are valuable resources for the Sabbath, family home evenings, holiday devotionals, and times of special need or celebration, such as at the time of a birth, death, or other life transition. Whether the music comes from our heart as we sing and play or enters the heart as we listen, it can be transformative. Filling our home with sacred music—ranging from Tabernacle Choir and other religious recordings to good classical music—helps create sacred time in our home on Sundays or holidays. Singing beloved hymns and carols with my family has become one of my greatest joys and helps keep the Sabbath, Christmas, and Easter Christ-centered.

Like many other members of the Church, I have personally experienced the same power of music in my personal life that the First Presidency described in the hymnbook's preface:

"In addition to blessing us as Church and family members, the hymns can greatly benefit us as individuals. Hymns can lift our spirits, give us courage, and move us to righteous action. They can fill our souls with heavenly thoughts and bring us a spirit of peace."[43]

What the First Presidency has taught about the power of hymns applies to all good music, which allows it to be a fundamental part of our worship. Because I have found it a natural way to express my feelings for God, I love the psalmist's expression,

> *I will sing unto the Lord as long as I live:*
> *I will sing praise to my God while I have my being. (Psalm 104:33)*

Just as a sacrament hymn prepares us for renewing our covenants, listening to beautiful music or gently singing a hymn can help us prepare to pray. Sometimes I find that a choice hymn or beloved song can convey my thoughts and deepest feelings to the Lord better than can prayer alone. The texts of sacred music are filled with the same peace, truth, and power that I find in the scriptures. But above all, such music can make any place and time sacred, transporting me higher. As with other forms of worship, musical spiritual experiences always leave me changed, inspired, strengthened, and more eager to do the Lord's will.

Conclusion

MAKING WORSHIP MORE MEANINGFUL
Finding Renewed Joy and Inspiration as We Seek God

> *This is the day which the Lord hath made;*
> *we will rejoice and be glad in it. . . .*
> *Thou art my God, and I will praise thee:*
> *thou art my God, I will exalt thee.*
> *O give thanks unto the Lord; for he is good:*
> *for his mercy endureth for ever.*
> —Psalm 118:24–29

From these most common and important ways of worshipping, we may conclude that at its heart worship is characterized by displays of sincere reverence arising from genuine love for God. Much of how we worship is drawn directly from biblical roots, building upon the patterns of ancient Israel in the Old Testament and the first Christians in the New Testament. Though we learn many of these patterns of worship directly from these texts, our current practices have also drawn heavily from Christian tradition. Strong parallels with Rabbinic Judaism and Islam show that worship is natural, that all men and women are drawn to seek an encounter with God that can change and improve their lives. The details of their practices may differ from our own, but Lutheran bishop Krister Stendahl's principle of holy envy suggests that we can and should be inspired by their devotion. Indeed, since worship goes back to

Adam and Eve, we know that it is the result of the natural yearning of children to seek a Parent who loves, cares, and provides for them.

The ways we show our reverence as we worship differ depending upon the situation or how we are worshipping. Prayer is often accompanied by physical signs of deference such as bowing our heads and kneeling, yet singing may manifest itself in joy, even exuberance. We may show reverence for a holy place through silence, whispered voices, and gentle actions, yet scripture study and discussion may vary from quiet contemplation to eager discovery. Ordinances are characterized by exactness and respect, and while both ritual and sacred experiences deserve careful observance and care, they should also bring joy. Worship is about reverence; it should not be about anxiety or fear in its negative sense. What makes the biblical expression "the fear of the Lord" about awe and wonder is love. We do not just worship God because he is great—we are drawn to him because he loves us, and we love him.

Doing Better What We Already Do Well

As Latter-day Saints, we have already been well taught and trained how to worship. We pray and participate in ordinances. We try to show reverence for holy places, keep the Sabbath, and celebrate other sacred times. We study the scriptures and love sacred music. In most cases, improving and deepening our worship is more about doing better what we already do well. We may simply need to be more deliberate about how we worship, trying harder to keep God as its focus. Effective worship requires preparation, which includes taking the time to recall God's power and love while being humble and repentant as we approach him. In these ways we create mental and spiritual space for worship, putting him first and preparing ourselves to be changed by him. True worship requires intentionality, not only worshipping with purpose and intent but also cultivating the ability to feel that we are actually in his presence.

Transformative worship requires mindfulness, which means being aware of how the Spirit is trying to change us. However, we should always remember Jesus' counsel to Nicodemus: "The wind bloweth where it listeth, and thou hearest the sound thereof, but canst not tell whence it cometh, and whither it goeth: so is every one that is born of the Spirit" (John 3:8). Because the Greek word for wind (Greek, *pneuma*) also means "spirit," we must remember that we cannot force the Spirit, predetermining when and how we will feel it. Sometimes mindfulness means waiting upon the Lord, taking the time to listen to how he is trying to speak to us and accepting his direction even when it is not what we expect or want.

Worship is, in the end, a personal matter. While some of our most fulfilling worship occurs in our families or in communities of faith, even in these settings the responsibility lies with us to make the experience true worship. Whether alone or with others, we must make sure we are worshipping with both our hearts and our minds and not just going through the motions. To deepen our devotion further, we must resolve to make the words we speak, the actions we perform, the places and times we honor, the texts we study, and the songs we sing have meaning. As we do that, we can experience God's Spirit in greater measure, strengthening and enabling us to serve him with all our strength.

Loving God by Serving Others

"For I was an hungred, and ye gave me meat: I was thirsty, and ye gave me drink: I was a stranger, and ye took me in: naked, and ye clothed me: I was sick, and ye visited me: I was in prison, and ye came unto me. . . . Verily I say unto you, Inasmuch as ye have done it unto one of the least of these my brethren, ye have done it unto me" (Matthew 25:35-40).

Worshipping God with our strength presupposes action. It is not enough simply to worship individually and then passively enjoy the spirit that follows. Nor is it enough to see the fruit of worship in increased individual obedience or improved personal conduct. While we have not considered every possible way that we worship the Lord, one culminating way of worshipping God that deserves mention is loving service of others. As King Benjamin taught, "When ye are in the service of your fellow beings ye are only in the service of your God" (Mosiah 2:17). God has always taught his people to care for each other, especially for those of us who are poor, disadvantaged, or struggling. Accordingly, the law of Moses protected the widow, orphan, and stranger, and both Hebrew and Nephite prophets called upon believers to help the poor and eschew pride, greed, and violence.[1] But above all, the example of Jesus and his teachings calls upon us to love and care for each other. While loving God with all our hearts, souls, minds, and strength is the first commandment, the second, that we should love our neighbor, is like unto it (Mark 12:30–31; parallels Matthew 22:37–39; Luke 10:27). Indeed, we often keep the first commandment by keeping the second.

This impulse to help others is found among believers everywhere. As we have seen, after the destruction of the Jerusalem Temple, the Jewish sages determined that ritual sacrifice could be replaced with prayer and with acts of loving kindness. A prime form of such loving kindness is charity (Hebrew, *ṣedaqah*), which means "righteousness," because giving of one's means, time, or concern is a righteous act.[2] Similarly, one of the Five Pillars of Islam is almsgiving (Arabic, *zakāt*). The Muslim practice involves "spending for the sake of God" and implies that by helping others, one is actually giving back to God what was his all along.[3] Inspired by the teachings of Jesus, Christians throughout the ages have sought to care for the poor, the sick, and the afflicted. Mother Teresa famously taught that in the poor she saw the face of God,[4] which is a striking modern example of the truth that King Benjamin taught. If one of the objectives of worship is to encounter God, then serving others is an important way of accomplishing that.

Our word *charity*, of course, is not limited to helping others with our means. We should never "suffer that the beggar putteth up his petition to [us] in vain" (Mosiah 4:16), but while we should always give the needy something, depending upon our capacity, the situation, and inspiration, our giving may range from a meal to a handout of money, a smile, or a silent prayer. Above all, someone in need of help, small or great, ought to be treated lovingly as a human being. Ultimately, no matter how we give, our giving changes *us,* which is the objective of worship. As "the pure love of Christ," charity includes loving Christ purely, having the kind of love that he has, and loving those whom he loves (Moroni 7:47).[5] But charity is also a gift of the Spirit. Mormon wrote, "Pray unto the Father with all the energy of heart, that ye may be filled with this love, which he hath bestowed upon all who are true followers of his Son, Jesus Christ; that ye may become the sons of God; that when he shall appear we shall be like him, for we shall see him as he is; that we may have this hope; that we may be purified even as he is pure" (Moroni 7:48). Worshipping, especially worshipping by serving others, purifies us and promises us a greater, more wonderful transformation.

Changed from Glory into Glory

Each act of worship has the potential to soften, comfort, and change our hearts and then empower us to do something here and now. These changes are some of the practical, immediate effects of real worship. Inasmuch as our goal is a daily life of worship, these changes should continue throughout our lives. Nevertheless, the ultimate purpose of worship is to receive eternal life and share it forever with God, Christ, and those whom we love.

One of my favorite traditional hymns is "Love Divine, All Love Excelling," by Charles Wesley. The moving lyrics of this hymn speak of Jesus' visiting us with salvation, taking away our desire for sinning, and giving us his life, all of which lead us to an eternal life of prayer and praise:

> *Love divine, all love excelling,*
> *Joy of heaven, to earth come down;*
> *Fix in us thy humble dwelling;*
> *All thy faithful mercies crown!*
> *Jesus, Thou art all compassion,*
> *Pure unbounded love Thou art;*

Visit us with Thy salvation;
Enter every trembling heart.

Breathe, O breathe Thy loving Spirit,
Into every troubled breast!
Let us all in Thee inherit;
Let us find that second rest.
Take away our love of sinning;
Alpha and Omega be;
End of faith, as its Beginning,
Set our hearts at liberty.

Come, Almighty, to deliver,
Let us all Thy life receive;
Suddenly return, and never,
Never more Thy temples leave.
Thee we would be always blessing,
Serve Thee as Thy hosts above,
Pray and praise Thee without ceasing,
Glory in Thy perfect love.

Finish, then, Thy new creation;
Pure and spotless let us be.
Let us see Thy great salvation
Perfectly restored in Thee;
Changed from glory into glory,
Till in heaven we take our place,
Till we cast our crowns before Thee,
Lost in wonder, love, and praise.[6]

This hymn has been beautifully arranged by Mack Wilberg,[7] and I have had the privilege of singing it many times with the Tabernacle Choir and Orchestra at Temple Square. Without fail it is a moving, worshipful experience. It captures for me so much of what worship is about, portraying it as our loving response to Jesus' faithful mercy and unbounded love. It illustrates the effects of the Spirit that accompanies worship and how it comforts and sanctifies us. With an allusion to Jesus coming to his temples—both physical temples and each of us as part of the body of Christ—it reminds me of the ordinances that bring eternal life. It points my mind forward to the ultimate objective of worship, which is to bring us pure and spotless into his presence. There, changed from glory into glory, we will experience eternal joy in worship that will never end.

NOTES

INTRODUCTION: WHAT IS WORSHIP?

1. "-ship" and "Worship," *Oxford Dictionary of English Etymology,* 821, 1013.
2. McConkie, "How to Worship," 167; Tozer, *Purpose of Man,* 61, 75–77; Block, *For the Glory of God,* 1.
3. "Adorō," *Oxford Latin Dictionary,* 53; "Adore," *Oxford Dictionary of English Etymology,* 14.
4. In his examination of the biblical theology of worship, David Peterson of Oak Hill Theological College in London suggests that at the heart of worship is engaging with God, spiritually meeting and interacting with him (*Engaging with God,* 19–20, 238–41, 283–85).
5. Wilberg, "His Voice as the Sound," in *My Song in the Night.*
6. Only the first verse appears in most early versions of "His Voice as the Sound of a Dulcimer Sweet." Instead, it appears as a so-called "wandering verse" in many early folk hymns. For instance, it appears as verse 7 in the 1859 hymn "O Thou, in Whose Presence My Soul Takes Delight" (*Baptist Hymn Book,* no. 948), whose verses 8–10 also provided Wilberg with the rest of the lyrics for his arrangement.
7. This direction, known as the *Shema* because of the opening command "to hear" (Hebrew, *šəma'*), is considered the fundamental Jewish article of faith, being the first confession a child is taught to say and the last a

NOTES

dying person strives to utter. Millgram, *Jewish Worship,* 96–101, 397–99; Donin, *To Pray as a Jew,* 144–45, 148–56.

8. "Ḥwh" and "Šḥh," *Brown-Driver-Briggs Hebrew and English Lexicon,* 1005–6; "Proskyneō," *Greek-English Lexicon,* 882–83.
9. Uchtdorf, "Gift of Grace," 109.
10. Jacob 4:5; D&C 18:40; 20:19, 29. See McConkie, "Lord God of the Restoration," 51; "Worship," *Encyclopedia of Mormonism,* 4:1596.
11. Revelation 5:8–14; 3 Nephi 11:17, 19; 19:18–23; D&C 76:21. President Gordon B. Hinckley said: "He is the Savior and the Redeemer of the world. I believe in Him. I declare His divinity without equivocation or compromise. I love Him. I speak His name in reverence and wonder. I worship Him as I worship His Father, in spirit and in truth. I thank Him and kneel before His wounded feet and hands and side, amazed at the love He offers me" ("Father, Son, and Holy Ghost," 51).
12. See Genesis 3:23–24; 2 Nephi 2:19–20; Alma 42:9; D&C 29:41–44.
13. Packer, "Reverence Invites Revelation," 21–23.
14. "Yārē'," *Brown-Driver-Briggs Hebrew and English Lexicon,* 431; "Yārē'," *Theological Dictionary of the Old Testament,* 6:290–315; "Phobeō," *Greek-English Lexicon,* 1060–62; "Phobeomai," *Theological Dictionary of the New Testament,* 9:189–219, especially 201–3 and 208–13; "Phobeomai," *Exegetical Dictionary of the New Testament,* 3:429–32; Webber, *Worship,* 30; Peterson, *Engaging with God,* 70–72. Other words connoting feelings ranging from dread to awe include *gûr* and *pāḥaḏ* in Hebrew and *saleuō* in Greek.
15. Rabbinic Judaism required that the worshipper "know before Whom you are standing" and directed that "he who prays must direct his heart to heaven" (*Babylonian Talmud, Berakot* 28b, 31a, as cited in Millgram, *Jewish Worship,* 25–26).
16. Donin, *To Pray as a Jew,* 19.
17. "Intendō," *Oxford Latin Dictionary,* 937–38; "Intend," *Oxford Dictionary of English Etymology,* 479–80. Verena Ursenbach Hatch (1922–2012), a Latter-day Saint musician and author, noted about prayer: "*Man reaches upward and seeks audience with God* through prayer, and often through prayer and fasting. Actual communion comes as a result of man's *search* for God's presence" (*Worship and Music,* 4; emphasis added).
18. Runes, *Dictionary of Philosophy,* 164; "Intentionality," *Stanford Encyclopedia*

of Philosophy, accessed January 31, 2015, http://plato.stanford.edu/archives/win2014/entries/intentionality.

19. The concept of mindfulness is found both in Buddhist meditation (see Gunaratana, *Mindfulness in Plain English*) and in cognitive and behavioral therapy in psychology (see Van Vreeswijk et al., *Mindfulness*). I use "mindfulness" in the simple, broad sense of (1) being aware of what we are doing when we act and (2) seeking to understand how our actions are affecting us and those around us.
20. Millgram, *Jewish Worship*, 25, notes, "The term *holiness*, though elusive, is nonetheless indispensable to ideal worship. To be in a state of holiness implies an awareness of the mysterious and godly."
21. Neiger, "To Act in Holiness before the Lord," 2.
22. *Svenska kyrkans tidning*, July 11, 1985, as cited in Wirthlin, "Pulling in the Gospel Net," 60; Landau, "Interview with Krister Stendahl," 31; Martin, "Krister Stendahl," *New York Times*, April 16, 2008; "Vår Och Andras Tro," Mormon Lady Blog, accessed October 7, 2015, http://mormonlady.se/2011/08/04/var-och-andras-tro/.

CHAPTER 1. PRAYER

1. Zaleski and Zaleski, *Prayer*, 15–32.
2. "Pray," *Oxford Dictionary of English Etymology*, 703; "Precor," *Oxford Latin Dictionary*, 1451.
3. Eyring, "Exhort Them to Pray," 4; emphasis added.
4. Donin, *To Be a Jew*, 18. Regarding proper preparation for prayer, Millgram, *Jewish Worship*, 29, relates a conversation with the Hasidic Tzanzer Rebbe: "'What does the Rebbe do before praying?' 'I pray,' said he, 'that I may be able to pray properly.'"
5. Millgram, *Jewish Worship*, 9.
6. *Hymns*, no. 145, vv. 1–2.
7. Kierkegaard, *Purity of Heart Is to Will One Thing*, 23. Douglas V. Steere translates the full quotation more literally as "a hasty explanation could assert that to pray is a useless act, because a man's prayer does not alter the unalterable. . . . The prayer does not change God, but it changes the one who offers it. It is the same with the substance of what is spoken. Not God, but you, the maker of the confession, get to know something by your act of confession."

NOTES

8. Donin, *To Pray as a Jew,* 4.
9. Ezra knelt and stretched his hands up to God (Ezra 9:5), a posture also attested by Solomon (1 Kings 8:22), the people in Isaiah's time (Isaiah 1:15), and the psalmist (Psalm 141:2). In Nehemiah 8:5–6 the people combine all of these actions, standing, lifting their hands, bowing their heads, and bowing. See Seely and Chadwick, *Ascending the Mountain of the Lord,* " 106–11, 117, 123–24, 127.
10. McConkie, "Why the Lord Ordained Prayer," 14.
11. See Genesis 2:16–17, 23–24; 3:8–19; compare Moses 3:16–17, 23–24; 4:14–25.
12. See the examples of Noah (Genesis 6:13–7:5); Abraham (Genesis 15:1–6); Moses (Exodus 3:1–4:17; 33:11); Samuel (1 Samuel 3:4–9); David (1 Samuel 23:2–4); Solomon (1 Kings 3:5–14); Isaiah (Isaiah 6:1–13); and Jeremiah (Jeremiah 1:4–19).
13. See "Psalms, Book of," *Anchor Bible Dictionary,* 5:531–34; deClaissé-Walford, Jacobson, and Tanner, *Book of Psalms,* 19–21.
14. Vulliamy, "Let's Roll," *Guardian,* December 1, 2001.
15. Luke, for instance, emphasized how Jesus prayed at his baptism (Luke 3:21), all night before the call of the Twelve Apostles (Luke 6:12), at the Transfiguration (Luke 9:28–29), at Gethsemane (Luke 22:41–46), and on the cross (Luke 23:46). Besides these examples of prayer at pivotal moments in his life, Jesus called upon us to pray always (see Luke 18:1; 21:36).
16. "Tameion," *Greek-English Lexicon,* 988.
17. "Battalogeō," *Greek-English Lexicon,* 172; Nolland, *Gospel of Matthew,* 284–85. For the Latter-day Saint view of vain repetitions, see Asay, in *Prayer,* 39.
18. *A Message from The Church of Jesus Christ of Latter-day Saints,* a pamphlet reproduced as "Father, Consider Your Ways," 12.
19. "Peirasmos," *Greek-English Lexicon,* 793. Similarly, the petition "deliver us from evil" can be seen as a prayer not only to be delivered from the power of evil forces or powers but also to be spared from unfortunate mishaps or occurrences that can be so common in this fallen world.
20. Oaks, *In His Holy Name,* 18, 40.
21. "Homothymadon," *Greek-English Lexicon,* 706.
22. See, for example, Acts 2:1, 46; 4:24; 5:12; 15:25.

23. *Hymns,* no. 145, v. 6.
24. *Babylonian Talmud, Berakot* 6a, as cited in Donin, *To Pray as a Jew,* 14–15.
25. Donin, *To Be a Jew,* 159–60. See Millgram, *Jewish Worship,* 101–8; Donin, *To Pray as a Jew,* 69–108.
26. This was not only for practical reasons, such as building a sense of community and avoiding assimilation, but because Hebrew was the language of the prophets, of the Bible, and has been the sacred language for countless Jews through the ages. See Millgram, *Jewish Worship,* 34–35; Donin, *To Pray as a Jew,* 16–18.
27. *Babylonian Talmud, Berakot* 31a, as cited in Donin, *To Be a Jew,* 161; *To Pray as a Jew,* 19.
28. See Webber, *Worship,* 220–21.
29. White, *Introduction to Christian Worship,* 133.
30. White, *History of Christian Worship,* 83–85. For instance, in Western Europe during the Middle Ages, this daily office could consist of as many as eight services a day, beginning with Vespers at sunset, which was considered the end of one day and the start of the next; Compline before bed; Vigils or Matins in the very early morning while it was yet dark; Lauds at daybreak; Prime at about 7:00; Terce in the middle of the morning about 9:00; Sext at noon; and None in the middle of the afternoon about 3:00. See also Webber, *Worship,* 105.
31. Webber, *Worship,* 169.
32. Broderick, "Sign of the Cross," *Catholic Encyclopedia,* 553; http://www.newadvent.org/cathen/13785a.htm.
33. For the Muslim, worship also consists of living one's entire life in obedience to God. See Al-Ghazālī, *Inner Dimensions of Islamic Worship,* 8.
34. Turner, *Islam,* 137–41.
35. Turner, *Islam,* 145.
36. Al-Ghazālī, *Inner Dimensions of Islamic Worship,* 38–39.
37. White, *History of Christian Worship,* 117–18; *Introduction to Christian Worship,* 140–42.
38. Arguments against written prayers, not just in private but in services, pointed out that set prayers deprived worshipers of their own expressions, did not meet the needs of particular congregations, could lead to overfamiliarity and lack of interest, and, most of all, did not represent the appropriate approach to the Father. See Webber, *Worship,* 115.

39. *Hymns,* no. 145, v. 4.
40. White, *History of Christian Worship,* 120; *Introduction to Christian Worship,* 146.
41. Bushman, *Rough Stone Rolling,* 22–27; Harper, *Joseph Smith's First Vision,* 18–22.
42. *Histories, 1832–1844,* Joseph Smith Papers, 204–19. See Bushman, *Rough Stone Rolling,* 37–41; Harper, *Joseph Smith's First Vision,* 44–52.
43. Smith, *History of Joseph Smith by His Mother,* 47–48, records that Joseph's mother, Lucy Mack Smith, naturally turned to fervent prayer during a dangerous sickness. See also Bushman, *Rough Stone Rolling,* 11–14.
44. Harper, *Joseph Smith's First Vision,* 27–30.
45. Smith, *Teachings of the Prophet Joseph Smith,* 22; or *Journals, May 1843–June 1844,* Joseph Smith Papers, 63; emphasis added.
46. Hanks, in *Prayer,* 26–29.
47. Hanks, in *Prayer,* 23.
48. Hinckley, "Stone Cut Out of the Mountain," 84.
49. Ashton, in *Prayer,* 74.
50. Rector, in *Prayer,* 70.
51. Oaks, "Language of Prayer," 15–16.
52. See Kimball, *Faith Precedes the Miracle,* 201; *Prayer,* 38–39, 70; Oaks, "Language of Prayer," 16. For connections between the idiom of the King James Bible and Restoration scripture, see Barlow, *Mormons and the Bible,* 27; Jackson, *King James Bible and the Restoration,* 182–95.
53. "Family Prayer," *Encyclopedia of Mormonism,* 2:498–99; see also *Preach My Gospel,* 73.
54. Bednar, "Pray Always," 42–44.
55. Eyring, "Prayer of Faith," 4.
56. "Prayer," LDS Bible Dictionary, 752–53.
57. McConkie, "Why the Lord Ordained Prayer," 14–15.

CHAPTER 2. ORDINANCES AND OTHER RITUALS

1. The word *ordinance* comes from the Latin verb *ordinō,* meaning not only "to set in order or arrange" but also "to rule, govern, or appoint" (*Oxford Latin Dictionary,* 1265–66). *Ordinance* also has a broader meaning that includes an authoritative decree or teaching as well as a prescribed usage, practice, or ceremony.

NOTES

2. Brown, *First Principles and Ordinances*, 68–69, 79–86.
3. "Rītus," *Oxford Latin Dictionary*, 1656; "Rite," *Oxford Dictionary of English Etymology*, 769.
4. See Belnap, *By Our Rites of Worship*, 1–2.
5. White, *Introduction to Christian Worship*, 176.
6. See also Belnap, *By Our Rites of Worship*, 5.
7. Rojas, "Covenants and Ordinances," 44; Neuenschwander, "Ordinances and Covenants," 24.
8. Skinner, *Temple Worship*, 23–27.
9. *Joseph Smith* [manual], 474.
10. Dudley and Rowell, *Oil of Gladness*, 35–43, 60; Fleming, "Biblical Tradition of Anointing Priests," 402–13; "Washings and Anointings," *Encyclopedia of Mormonism*, 4:1551.
11. Oaks, "Keys and Authority of the Priesthood," 49–52.
12. "Qārēb" and "Qorbān," *Brown-Driver-Briggs Hebrew and English Lexicon*, 897–98. See Millgram, *Jewish Worship*, 51; Donin, *To Pray as a Jew*, 117–18.
13. Burnt offerings (Hebrew, *ʿōlāh*), Leviticus 1:1–17; grain offerings (Hebrew, *minḥāh;* KVJ, "meat offering"), Leviticus 2:1–16; peace offerings (Hebrew, *zebaḥ šəlāmîm*), Leviticus 3:1–17; purification offerings (Hebrew *ḥaṭṭāʾt;* KJV, "sin offerings"), Leviticus 4:1–5:13; reparation or guilt offerings (Hebrew *ʾāšām;* KJV, "trespass offerings"), Leviticus 5:14–6:7. For detailed discussions of each, see Kraus, *Worship in Israel*, 113–22; Hess, *Israelite Religions*, 186–90; and Holzapfel, Pike, and Seely, *Jehovah and the World of the Old Testament*, 113–15.
14. Jackson and Millet, *Genesis to 2 Samuel*, 153–72. For detailed discussions of the five principal kinds of sacrifices described in Leviticus, see Kraus, *Worship in Israel*, 113–22; Hess, *Israelite Religions*, 186–90; and Holzapfel, Pike, and Seely, *Jehovah and the World of the Old Testament*, 113–15.
15. White, *Introduction to Christian Worship*, 178; Brueggemann, *Worship in Ancient Israel*, 21.
16. See, for instance, 1 Samuel 15:55; Psalm 51:16–17; Isaiah 1:11–18; Jeremiah 6:19–20; 7:21–22; Hosea 6:6; Amos 5:21–24; and Micah 6:6–8.

NOTES

17. Seely, in Holzapfel and Wayment, *From the Last Supper through the Resurrection,* 94.
18. "Baptizō," *Greek-English Lexicon,* 164–65.
19. Block, *For the Glory of God,* 146; Brown, *First Principles and Ordinances,* 93–96.
20. See 2 Corinthians 5:21; Hebrews 4:15; 1 Peter 2:22; 1 John 3:5; D&C 45:4.
21. "Baptism," *Encyclopedia of Mormonism,* 1:93; Brown, *First Principles and Ordinances,* 97–101
22. Webber, *Worship,* 147–50.
23. See Brown, *First Principles and Ordinances,* 101–7.
24. These examples include converts at Pentecost (Acts 2:41); the Samaritans by Philip (Acts 8:12–13, 16); the Ethiopian eunuch (Acts 8:36–38); Saul (Acts 9:18); Cornelius and his household (Acts 10:47–48); Lydia and her household (Acts 16:15); the prison guard and his household in Philippi (Acts 16:33); Crispus and many Corinthians (Acts 18:8); and previous disciples of John the Baptist, who were now baptized "in the name of the Lord Jesus" (Acts 19:5). See Block, *For the Glory of God,* 146–50.
25. See Block, *For the Glory of God,* 154–67, 263–68; White, *History of Christian Worship,* 24–30; *Introduction to Christian Worship,* 179–80.
26. Holland, "This Do in Remembrance of Me," 67.
27. 1 Corinthians 11:25; Mark 14:24; parallel Matthew 26:28; Luke 22:20.
28. "Katangellō," *Greek-English Lexicon,* 515.
29. Note the inspired additions to the account in Mark: "Behold, this is for you to do in remembrance of my body; for as oft as ye do this *ye will remember this hour that I was with you,*" and "as oft as ye do this ordinance, *ye will remember me in this hour that I was with you* and drank with you of this cup, even the last time in my ministry" (Joseph Smith Translation, Mark 14:21, 24; emphasis added).
30. Although the references to the bread and wine of the sacrament are clear, this declaration can also be taken metaphorically, with eating representing the wholehearted acceptance of Jesus and the necessity of his sacrificial death that brings eternal life to believers. See Wayment and Wilson, *Celebrating Easter,* 88, 104–6.
31. See Isaiah 25:6–8; Ezekiel 39:17–20; Zechariah 9:15; D&C 27:4–14.

NOTES

32. For the bestowal of the Holy Ghost, see the confirmation of the Samaritans (Acts 8:17–18) and the Ephesians (Acts 19:6) and perhaps Hebrews 6:2. For the conferral of authority and gifts, equivalent to our ordaining or setting apart, see the setting apart of the seven "deacons" of the Jerusalem church (Acts 6:6); the setting apart of Barnabas and Saul (Acts 13:3); Timothy's position as *presbyteros,* or elder (1 Timothy 4:14) and his unspecified "gift of God" (2 Timothy 1:6), which could have been either his receiving the Holy Ghost or his priesthood ordination. See "Laying On of Hands," *Encyclopedia of Mormonism,* 2:813–14.
33. For Jesus, see Mark 5:23 (parallel Matthew 9:28); 6:5 (parallel Luke 4:40); 7:32; 8:23; Luke 13:13. In the apostolic commission in Mark, Jesus directed his disciples that "they shall lay hands on the sick, and they shall recover" (Mark 16:18). For the laying on of hands by Jesus' followers, see signs and wonders by the apostles (Acts 5:16; see also 14:2; 19:11); the healing of Saul by Ananias (Acts 9:17, which is also connected with his being filled with the Holy Ghost); and the healing of the father of Publius by Paul on Malta (Acts 28:8).
34. See Dudley and Rowell, *Oil of Gladness,* 46–59.
35. *Babylonian Talmud,* Hagigah 27a, as cited in Donin, *To Be a Jew,* 101.
36. The rabbis who helped reformulate Judaism after the destruction of the temple in A.D. 70 found hope in the fact that Hebrew (see Hosea 6:6; emphasis added; cf. Amos 5:21–24; Micah 6:6–8). See Donin, *To Be a Jew,* 41–48.
37. For example, see Donin, *To Be a Jew,* 106–7 (for *šeḥitah,* or ritual slaughter), 125–27, 137–38 (for *taharat hamišpaḥah,* or "family purity laws," including *miqveh* baths), and 273–76 (for *brît milāh,* or ritual circumcision).
38. Donin, *To Be a Jew,* 101.
39. "Grace, sacramental," *New Catholic Encyclopedia,* 6:680–81; "Sacraments, theology of," *New Catholic Encyclopedia,* 12:812–13.
40. See White, *History of Christian Worship,* 44–52; *Introduction to Christian Worship,* 203–12. Justification for infant baptism was found in the earlier Jewish practice of circumcising infant males on the eighth day and Peter's invitation to baptism that suggested that the gospel promise was "unto you, and to your children" (Acts 2:38–39). See Webber, *Worship,* 154.

NOTES

41. See "Eucharistia" and "Charis," *Greek-English Lexicon*, 416 and 1079–81; "Eucharisteō," *Theological Dictionary of the New Testament*, 9:407–15; "Eucharist," *Oxford Dictionary of English Etymology*, 330.
42. See White, *History of Christian Worship*, 55–61, 79–81; *Introduction to Christian Worship*, 229–43.
43. "Confirm," *Oxford Dictionary of English Etymology*, 203; "Confirmō," *Oxford Latin Dictionary*, 400–401. See also White, *History of Christian Worship*, 83; *Introduction to Christian Worship*, 212–13; Webber, *Worship*, 54–55.
44. White, *Introduction to Christian Worship*, 185; J. R. Quinn, "Sacraments, Theology of," *New Catholic Encyclopedia*, 12:812–13.
45. White, *Introduction to Christian Worship*, 181; "Sacrament," *Oxford Dictionary of English Etymology*, 780–81; "Sacramentum," *Oxford Latin Dictionary*, 1674–75. See also Neuenschwander, "Ordinances and Covenants," 22.
46. Turner, *Islam*, 142–44.
47. See Al-Ghazālī, *Inner Dimensions of Islamic Worship*, 35
48. Turner, *Islam*, 92–95.
49. See Al-Ghazālī, *Inner Dimensions of Islamic Worship*, 45; Turner, *Islam*, 18.
50. White, *Introduction to Christian Worship*, 188.
51. White, *History of Christian Worship*, 107–16, 120–27, 132–34; *Introduction to Christian Worship*, 188. See also Neuenschwander, "Ordinances and Covenants," 22, and Wainwright and Tucker, *Oxford History of Christian Worship*, 317–33.
52. Allen and Leonard, *Story of the Latter-day Saints*, 49–50; Bushman, *Rough Stone Rolling*, 74–77.
53. See Mosiah 3:11–12, 16; 15:25; Moroni 8:19–25; D&C 20:71–72; 29:46–47.
54. When the Church was formally organized on April 6, 1830, many of those who had previously been baptized for the remission of sins were baptized again (see Barrett, *Joseph Smith and the Restoration*, 129, 131). This action paralleled how Nephite disciples who had previously been baptized were baptized again into the new church that the risen Lord organized among them (see 3 Nephi 19:10–12; 26:17, 21).
55. Millet et al., *LDS Beliefs*, 64.
56. Petersen, in *Prayer*, 61–62; Oaks, *In His Holy Name*, 37–39.

57. The precise date of the restoration of the Melchizedek Priesthood is still debated. See Barrett, *Joseph Smith and the Restoration*, 125–26; Allen and Leonard, *Story of the Latter-day Saints*, 50; Bushman, *Rough Stone Rolling*, 79–80.
58. Allen and Leonard, *Story of the Latter-day Saints*, 54; Bushman, *Rough Stone Rolling*, 109–10; Millet et al., *LDS Beliefs*, 126.
59. Millet et al., *LDS Beliefs*, 258–59.
60. Packer, "Gift of the Holy Ghost," 46–48.
61. Allen and Leonard, *Story of the Latter-day Saints*, 54; Bushman, *Rough Stone Rolling*, 109–10.
62. "Sacrament Prayers," *Encyclopedia of Mormonism*, 3:1244–45.
63. Oaks, *In His Holy Name*, 63–67; Millet et al., *LDS Beliefs*, 549.
64. Marriott, "Yielding Our Hearts to God," 31–32.
65. Neuenschwander, "Ordinances and Covenants," 25–26.
66. For the restoration of the various priesthood offices, see Barrett, *Joseph Smith and the Restoration*, 129, 167, 223, 294–99; Allen and Leonard, *Story of the Latter-day Saints*, 54, 88–92; Bushman, *Rough Stone Rolling*, 109–10, 154–55, 254–58.
67. Millet et al., *LDS Beliefs*, 501–3.
68. "Washings and Anointings," *Encyclopedia of Mormonism*, 4:1551; Bushman, *Rough Stone Rolling*, 310–15, 318; Anderson and Bergera, *Joseph Smith's Quorum of the Anointed*, xiv–xvii; Allen and Leonard, *Story of the Latter-day Saints*, 109–11.
69. Allen and Leonard, *Story of the Latter-day Saints*, 111. See Oaks, "Keys and Authority of the Priesthood," 50–51.
70. Allen and Leonard, *Story of the Latter-day Saints*, 184; Bushman, *Rough Stone Rolling*, 448–52, 497; Anderson and Bergera, *Joseph Smith's Quorum of the Anointed*, xx–xxix, who suggests a date different from Allen and Leonard's.
71. *Discourses of Brigham Young*, 416. See also Bushman, *Rough Stone Rolling*, 448–52, 497; Skinner, *Temple Worship*, 60–65; Millet et al., *LDS Beliefs*, 182–86.
72. Bednar, "Honorably Hold a Name and Standing," 98.
73. Skinner, *Temple Worship*, 40–41, 74–75, 92; Millet et al., *LDS Beliefs*, 503–4.

NOTES

CHAPTER 3. HOLY PLACES

1. Cannon, *Secret Language of Sacred Places*, 27–37.
2. Elder Jeffrey R. Holland noted, "I do not know the details of what happened on this planet before that, but I do know these two were created under the divine hand of God, that for a time they lived alone in a paradisiacal setting where there was neither human death nor future family, and that through a sequence of choices they transgressed a commandment of God which required that they leave their garden setting but which allowed them to have children before facing physical death" ("Where Justice, Love, and Mercy Meet," 105).
3. "Templum," *Oxford Latin Dictionary*, 1914–15; "Temple," *Oxford Dictionary of English Etymology*, 908. See Skinner, *Temple Worship*, 1–3; Millet et al., *LDS Beliefs*, 612.
4. Nibley, *Temple and Cosmos*, 19–23.
5. See "Temple," *Eerdmans Dictionary of the Bible*, 1280.
6. Orson Pratt, in *Journal of Discourses*, 18:343.
7. "Adam-ondi-Ahman," *Encyclopedia of Mormonism*, 1:19–20.
8. Block, *For the Glory of God*, 299–300. Isaac established an altar at Beersheba, where he saw the Lord (Genesis 26:23–25), as did Jacob at Shechem (Genesis 33:20).
9. Seely and Chadwick, *Ascending the Mountain of the Lord*, 394.
10. "Temple," LDS Bible Dictionary, 734.
11. Block, *For the Glory of God*, 300–302.
12. These rituals included changing the bread on the table of shewbread, which represented God's presence; lighting the lamps of the menorah, a seven-branched candelabrum that symbolized God's light and was also reminiscent of Eden's tree of life; and offering prayers at the golden altar of incense before the veil.
13. See Seely and Chadwick, *Ascending the Mountain of the Lord*, 13–18, 69–73. Interestingly, some of the high priest's vestments were also made of these colors (Exodus 28:4–8), suggesting that not only did his holy garments represent the authority with which he was clothed but they also connected him closely with the sacred space of the temple even when he was not inside it (Josephus, *Antiquities*, 3.7.7 [§180–85]; *Wars*, 5.5.7 [§232]; Philo, *On Flight and Finding*, §110). See Nibley, *Temple and Cosmos*, 80.

14. Holzapfel, Pike, and Seely, *Jehovah and the World of the Old Testament*, 104–7; Block, *For the Glory of God*, 302–5; Seely and Chadwick, *Ascending the Mountain of the Lord*, 12–35.
15. Millgram, *Jewish Worship*, 63–66; Webber, *Worship*, 36–38; Block, *For the Glory of God*, 184–85.
16. Block, *For the Glory of God*, 317.
17. Holzapfel, Huntsman, and Wayment, *Jesus Christ and the World of the New Testament*, 158–61. Whereas the Nephites were specifically instructed to cease the traditional blood offerings of the law of Moses (3 Nephi 9:19), no clear direction to the Jerusalem Saints in regard to sacrifices is preserved, and some Jewish Christians continued to use blood offerings for vows and other purification ceremonies (see Acts 21:26).
18. See, for example, Acts 2:2; 10:9; 12:12; Romans 16:5, 23; 1 Corinthians 16:19; Colossians 4:15–16. See also Holzapfel, Huntsman, and Wayment, *Jesus Christ and the World of the New Testament*, 161, 205, 305–7.
19. Huntington, Whitchurch, and Judd, *New Testament Brought to Light*, 76–77, and 77n27.
20. Block, *For the Glory of God*, 321.
21. Armstrong, *Jerusalem*, 158, 169–70, 327–30, 366–67, 402–3.
22. Millgram, *Jewish Worship*, 79–80, 82–83; Webber, *Worship*, 36–38; Cannon, *Secret Language of Sacred Places*, 104–5.
23. Millgram, *Jewish Worship*, 289–319.
24. After the early house churches, little is known about Christian places of worship until Constantine made Christianity a legal religion in A.D. 313. That action allowed the church to own property and openly build its own places of worship. See Cannon, *Secret Language of Sacred Places*, 115.
25. White, *History of Christian Worship*, 71–72, 101–3; *Introduction to Christian Worship*, 91–96; Webber, *Worship*, 141–42; Cannon, *Secret Language of Sacred Places*, 116–17.
26. White, *Introduction to Christian Worship*, 103–7; Cannon, *Secret Language of Sacred Places*, 122–28.
27. Shalev-Hurvitz, *Holy Sites Encircled*, 8–9.
28. *Ka'ba* in Arabic literally means "square or cube" and describes the shape of the black shrine that the Qur'ān describes, among other titles, as being the house of Allāh (Arabic, *Bait Ullah*).
29. Frishman and Khan, *The Mosque*, 32; Turner, *Islam*, 14, 157.

30. Turner, *Islam*, 156–65.
31. Frishman and Khan, *The Mosque*, 11; Turner, *Islam*, 140. Other than the area around the Ka'ba itself, the first mosque was Muhammad's home in Medina, where early Muslims gathered to be led by the prophet in prayer. After initially having his followers pray towards Jerusalem, Muhammad changed the *qiblah*, or direction of prayer, towards Mecca and the Ka'ba, connecting all prayer to the place where heaven and earth met (see Turner, *Islam*, 26).
32. Webber, *Worship*, 143–44.
33. White, *History of Christian Worship*, 138–40; Webber, *Worship*, 144; Chappell, *Christ-Centered Worship*, 15–16; Cannon, *Secret Language of Sacred Places*, 134.
34. Barrett, *Joseph Smith and the Restoration*, 9–11; Allen and Leonard, *Story of the Latter-day Saints*, 10–15, 29; Bushman, *Rough Stone Rolling*, 36–37.
35. *Children's Songbook*, p. 95; words and music © Janice Kappy Perry. Used by permission.
36. Barrett, *Joseph Smith and the Restoration*, 129; Allen and Leonard, *Story of the Latter-day Saints*, 54; Bushman, *Rough Stone Rolling*, 109.
37. See "Meetinghouses," *Encyclopedia of Mormonism*, 2:876–78. See also Plewe, *Mapping Mormonism*, 160–63.
38. "Meetinghouse," *Encyclopedia of Mormonism*, 2:876.
39. Packer, "Reverence Invites Revelation," 22.
40. "History of LDS Temples," *Encyclopedia of Mormonism*, 4:1451.
41. Skinner, *Temple Worship*, 47–54, 79–88, 191–97.
42. Young, in *Journal of Discourses*, 3:372. See also Millet et al., *LDS Beliefs*, 600–601.
43. Allen and Leonard, *Story of the Latter-day Saints*, 183–84; Bushman, *Rough Stone Rolling*, 421–25.
44. Allen and Leonard, *Story of the Latter-day Saints*, 183–84, 377; Bushman, *Rough Stone Rolling*, 421–25; "History of LDS Temples," *Encyclopedia of Mormonism*, 4:1452. Although baptisms and initiatory ordinances were performed in the Endowment House constructed in Salt Lake City in 1855, vicarious endowments and sealings were not (see Brigham Young, in *Journal of Discourses*, 16:186).
45. Skinner, *Temple Worship*, 148–49.
46. Skinner, *Temple Worship*, 159–80.

NOTES

47. "Temple," LDS Bible Dictionary, 734.
48. "Dedications," *Encyclopedia of Mormonism*, 1:367.

CHAPTER 4. SACRED TIME

1. Webber, *Worship*, 217–19; White, *Introduction to Christian Worship*, 47–48.
2. *Alexander's Hymns*, no. 248, vv. 1–2, p. 244.
3. Donin, *To Pray as a Jew*, 10–11.
4. Donin, *To Be a Jew*, 61–65.
5. "Sabbath," *Oxford Dictionary of English Etymology*, 779; "Šabbāt," *Brown-Driver-Briggs Hebrew and English Lexicon*, 991–92.
6. Millgram, *Jewish Worship*, 191; Donin, *To Be a Jew*, 67–70; Block, *For the Glory of God*, 275–76.
7. Kimball, "The Sabbath—A Delight," 4–5.
8. Donin, *To Be a Jew*, 65–67; Block, *For the Glory of God*, 275.
9. Millgram, *Jewish Worship*, 199–205; Donin, *To Be a Jew*, 218–19, 239–40, 250–52; Block, *For the Glory of God*, 288–92.
10. Although Rosh Hashanah, or the Feast of the Trumpets, falls on the first day of the seventh month of the Jewish calendar (Leviticus 23:24; Numbers 29:1), it became known as "the beginning of the year" (Ezekiel 40:1) because according to tradition, it was the day that God created Adam and Eve. See Block, *For the Glory of God*, 290–92.
11. Millgram, *Jewish Worship*, 360–62; Donin, *To Be a Jew*, 246–49.
12. Block, *For the Glory of God*, 277–78.
13. See Huntsman, *Miracles of Jesus*, 60.
14. Block, *For the Glory of God*, 282–85.
15. White, *Introduction to Christian Worship*, 50–54; Block, *For the Glory of God*, 277–80.
16. Webber, *Worship*, 221–22.
17. *Alexander's Hymns*, no. 248, v. 3, p. 244.
18. Millgram, *Jewish Worship*, 161.
19. Donin, *To Be a Jew*, 72–80.
20. Millgram, *Jewish Worship*, 161–98; Donin, *To Be a Jew*, 74–75, 81–88; *To Pray as a Jew*, 256–62.
21. Millgram, *Jewish Worship*, 276–83; Donin, *To Be a Jew*, 263–66, 299–301, 304–10.
22. Donin, *To Be a Jew*, 169.

23. White, *History of Christian Worship*, 61–62.
24. Easter is mentioned only once in the King James Version of the Bible, at Acts 12:4, where it is actually a translation for "Passover." Nowhere do the scriptures actually mandate that we should celebrate the Savior's resurrection, his birth, or other events from his life. See Block, *For the Glory of God*, 293–94.
25. A Spanish pilgrim named Egeria, who made a pilgrimage to the Holy Land about A.D. 381–384, recorded how worshipers in Jerusalem retraced the final week of Jesus' life, beginning on the Mount of Olives and concluding with the resurrection on Easter morning at the Church of the Holy Sepulchre. See White, *Introduction to Christian Worship*, 55–56, 59–60; Farley, *Following Egeria*, 25–42, 48–52, 139–52.
26. See White, *History of Christian Worship*, 64–65; *Introduction to Christian Worship*, 61–62.
27. White, *Introduction to Christian Worship*, 61–64.
28. Turner, *Islam*, 143–44.
29. White, *Introduction to Christian Worship*, 64–66.
30. White, *History of Christian Worship*, 128.
31. Hinckley, "Wondrous and True Story of Christmas," 2.
32. See Huntsman, *God So Loved the World*, 1–5, 121–23; *Good Tidings of Great Joy*, 1–15, 135–37, 143–47.
33. "Sabbath Day," *Encyclopedia of Mormonism*, 3:1241.
34. Millet et al., *LDS Beliefs*, 547.
35. "Sabbath Day," *Encyclopedia of Mormonism*, 3:1241–42.
36. "Church Leaders Call for Better Observance of Sabbath Day," news release June 20, 2015, accessed July 25, 2015, http://www.mormonnewsroom.org/article/church-leaders-call-for-better-observance-of-sabbath-day.
37. Packer, "Reverence Invites Revelation," 22.
38. Petersen, "The Sabbath Day," 49.
39. Hill, "Five Ways to Celebrate the Sabbath As a Family."
40. Kimball, "The Sabbath—A Delight," 4–5.
41. Nelson, "Sabbath Is a Delight," 130.
42. "Fasting," *Encyclopedia of Mormonism*, 2:500–501.
43. "Sabbath Day," *Encyclopedia of Mormonism*, 3:1242.
44. *Hymns*, no. 138; text by John S. Tanner, © Intellectual Reserve, Inc. Used by permission.

45. Bednar, "More Diligent and Concerned at Home," 19–20.
46. *Alexander's Hymns*, no. 248, v. 4, p. 244.

CHAPTER 5. READING, PREACHING, AND TEACHING GOD'S WORD

1. Block, *For the Glory of God*, 169.
2. Chapell, *Christ-Centered Worship*, 220.
3. See http://www.neot-kedumim.org.il/.
4. The so-called Documentary Hypothesis examines the five books of the Pentateuch and on the basis of the use of the divine names of God, stylistic and diction differences, doublets or repetitions, thematic divergences, and other factors discerns four different original sources (known as J, E, P, and D) that were later woven together to give the Torah its current form. It is possible to accept many of the observations of the Documentary Hypothesis but still accept that there was some original Mosaic material that perhaps came down to the final editors in different forms or editorial strands. See Brown, "Approaches to the Pentateuch," 3–23; Holzapfel, Pike, and Seely, *Jehovah and the World of the Old Testament*, 144–45; and Bokovoy, *Authoring the Old Testament*.
5. "Yārāh > tôrāh," *Brown-Driver-Briggs Hebrew and English Lexicon*, 435–36.
6. See Block, *For the Glory of God*, 182.
7. Bandstra, *Reading the Old Testament*, 17–18.
8. Block, *For the Glory of God*, 181–83.
9. Block, *For the Glory of God*, 170–76, 337–38.
10. See Schmitt, "Prophecy (Preexilic Hebrew)," *Anchor Bible Dictionary*, 5:482; "Prophet," *Harper's Bible Dictionary*, 826; "Nābi,'" *Brown-Driver-Briggs Hebrew and English Lexicon*, 611–12; see "Prophet," LDS Bible Dictionary, 709.
11. Holzapfel, Pike, and Seely, *Jehovah and the World of the Old Testament*, 6, 10, 276. There may be another reason for their placement, however. Just as God revealed his will through his human prophets, so he often reveals his will through the events of history itself.
12. Holzapfel, Pike, and Seely, *Jehovah and the World of the Old Testament*, 6, 10.
13. Bandstra, *Reading the Old Testament*, 369–72.
14. "Ezra," *Anchor Bible Dictionary*, 2:726–28.

15. Millgram, *Jewish Worship*, 114–15.
16. Evans, *Fabricating Jesus*, 39–40.
17. Perhaps the best example of this kērygmatic preaching is the speech of Peter to Cornelius in Acts 10:36–43. See Judd, Huntsman, and Hopkin, *Ministry of Peter*, 177–82.
18. Jackson, *How the New Testament Came to Be*, 191–95, 203.
19. Millgram, *Jewish Worship*, 68–69, 70, 84, 111–20, 182–86; Donin, *To Be a Jew*, 165–66, 257.
20. Millgram, *Jewish Worship*, 15–16, 67–72; Block, *For the Glory of God*, 184–85.
21. Armstrong, *Jerusalem*, 156.
22. These important texts and commentaries include the Mishnah, which was compiled in A.D. 200 from traditions believed to have been handed down orally by the sages from the time of Moses, and the Talmud, which is composed of the Mishnah and centuries of rabbinic commentary on it. See Millgram, *Jewish Worship*, 125–29.
23. See Marcus, *Rituals of Childhood*, 7, 21–23, 58.
24. Webber, *Worship*, 164–69.
25. White, *History of Christian Worship*, 69–70; *Introduction to Christian Worship*, 154–57; Chappell, *Christ-Centered Worship*, 222–23.
26. Lane, *Christian Spirituality*, 20; Thompson and Howard, *Soul Feast*, 24.
27. Turner, *Islam*, 41–44, 61–67.
28. Webber, *Worship*, 110–14.
29. "Doctrine and Covenants," *Encyclopedia of Mormonism*, 1:404–7.
30. Benson, "Book of Mormon and the Doctrine and Covenants," 83–85.
31. Bednar, "Reservoir of Living Water," 3–7.
32. "Scripture Study," *Encyclopedia of Mormonism*, 3:1284–85.
33. Some of Block's suggestions for evangelical meetings might also be beneficial for our own meetings. These include not just using a verse or two in a talk or lesson to prove a point but reading longer passages to let scripture speak for itself; promote an attitude of reverence when reading scriptures, emphasizing by our tone and demeanor that they are important and represent the Lord's word; subordinate the talk or lesson to the scriptures, realizing that rarely are our words better than those of scripture (*For the Glory of God*, 190–92).
34. See, for example, *Preach My Gospel*, 180.

35. Ballard, "Pure Testimony," 41.
36. Hales, "Holy Scriptures," 26–27; emphasis added.

CHAPTER 6. WORSHIPPING GOD THROUGH MUSIC

1. Jessop, "Music and Mormons."
2. Hatch, *Worship and Music*, 56.
3. Block, *For the Glory of God*, 225–27.
4. Packer, "Inspiring Music—Worthy Thoughts," 25–27.
5. Block, *For the Glory of God*, 228.
6. deClaissé-Walford, Jacobson, and Tanner, *Book of Psalms*, 19–21, 39–43.
7. Bandstra, *Reading the Old Testament*, 392.
8. The sometimes enigmatic references in the headings of many of the psalms were performance directions. Hence instructions to the choirmaster (KJV, "chief musician") suggests choral performance, and references to stringed instruments (KJV, "on Neginoth") implies accompaniment. Likewise, some other mysterious terms may have referred to now-lost melodies. The word *selâ*, which sometimes appears in the middle of a psalm, was probably a musical direction, perhaps indicating that players should take up their instruments or that singers should repeat a section. See deClaissé-Walford, Jacobson, and Tanner, *Book of Psalms*, 12–13, 73n8; "Music and Musical Instruments," *Anchor Bible Dictionary*, 4:933.
9. Millgram, *Jewish Worship*, 362–63; Block, *For the Glory of God*, 228–29.
10. deClaissé-Walford, Jacobson, and Tanner, *Book of Psalms*, 401.
11. "*The Redeemer* Performed for Easter."
12. See Huntsman, *Good Tidings of Great Joy*, 58–59; see also Block, *For the Glory of God*, 231.
13. *Hallel* is short for *halelûyāh*, which means "praise *YHWH*." Psalms 112–14 were usually sung before the Passover meal, and Psalms 115–18 at its conclusion. See deClaissé-Walford, Jacobson, and Tanner, *Book of Psalms*, 847; Block, *For the Glory of God*, 231.
14. Like the canticles in Luke, these Greek texts are poetic, though the style is more similar to Hebrew poetry than to Greek. The vocabulary is different from that of the surrounding passages, and other features suggest that they are in fact liturgical hymns that Paul is quoting for his readers. The most commonly identified hymn fragments include Philippians 2:6–11; Colossians 1:15–20; Ephesians 1:3–14; Ephesians 2:14–16;

NOTES

Ephesians 5:14; 1 Timothy 3:16; 2 Timothy 2:11–13; Titus 3:4–7. See von Dehsen, "Hymnic Forms in the New Testament," 8.

15. The Trisagion, or "thrice-holy," expanded (Revelation 4:8–11; cf. Isaiah 6:3); Worthy Is the Lamb (Revelation 5:9–10, 12, 13); The Kingdom of Our Lord (Revelation 11:15–17); The Song of Moses (Revelation 15:3–4); The Marriage of the Lamb (Revelation 19:6–7); Jesus' Song of Himself, Our Response (Revelation 22:16–17).
16. Block, *For the Glory of God*, 234–36.
17. Millgram, *Jewish Worship*, 29, 363–65; Donin, *To Pray as a Jew*, 20–21.
18. Sefer Ḥasidim 11, as cited in Donin, *To Pray as a Jew*, 21.
19. Millgram, *Jewish Worship*, 518–24; Donin, *To Be a Jew*, 195–97.
20. Millgram, *Jewish Worship*, 366; Donin, *To Pray as a Jew*, 21–22.
21. Although Augustine, *Enarrationes in Psalmos*, 72.1, is often cited for this quotation (see White, *Introduction to Christian Worship*, 112), the passage actually says, "Anyone who sings praise is not only praising, but praising cheerfully. The singer of praise is not only performing musically but showing love for the one who is sung about" (Augustine, *Exposition of the Psalms*, III.17.470).
22. White, *History of Christian Worship*, 70–71, 100–101; *Introduction to Christian Worship*, 119–21; Webber, *Worship*, 197–99.
23. Shiloah, *Music in the World of Islam*, 31–44; Turner, *Islam*, 138, 183–84; see also Maurer, "Music in the World of Islam."
24. Webber, *Worship*, 199.
25. Hatch, *Worship and Music*, 102–4; White, *History of Christian Worship*, 136–37, 172; *Introduction to Christian Worship*, 121–23; Wolff, *Johann Sebastian Bach*, 237–304.
26. Stackhouse, "Hymnody and Politics," 45–47.
27. *Hymns*, nos. 119, 192, and 201; see also nos. 31, 74, 79, 88, 90, 147, and 317.
28. White, *History of Christian Worship*, 137–38; *Introduction to Christian Worship*, 123–26.
29. *Hymns*, nos. 66 and 200; see also nos. 102, 118, 209, and 217.
30. White, *History of Christian Worship*, 136–37; *Introduction to Christian Worship*, 121, 127.
31. Wolff, *Johann Sebastian Bach*, xxvii, 463, 467.
32. Wolff, *Johann Sebastian Bach*, 5.

NOTES

33. Wilberg, *Come, Ye Thankful People, Come.*
34. *Westminster Hymnal*, no. 265, vv. 3–4, p. 250.
35. White, *History of Christian Worship*, 173; *Introduction to Christian Worship*, 127–28.
36. Hicks, *Mormonism and Music*, 2–4.
37. Hicks, *Mormonism and Music*, 10.
38. Hatch, *Worship and Music*, 119–23; Hicks, *Mormonism and Music*, 10, 19–20, 109, 121, 123, 130–31.
39. *Hymns*, ix.
40. Hicks, *Mormon Tabernacle Choir*, 17–25, 89–92, 160–62.
41. Much earlier, President Packer taught, "An organist who has the sensitivity to quietly play prelude music from the hymnbook tempers our feelings and causes us to go over in our minds the lyrics which teach the peaceable things of the kingdom" ("Reverence Invites Revelation," 22).
42. *Hymns*, x.
43. *Hymns*, x.

CONCLUSION: MAKING WORSHIP MORE MEANINGFUL

1. See, for example, Exodus 22:22–27; Deuteronomy 10:18; 15:7–11; 24:14–22; 26:12–13; Isaiah 1:17; 3:14–15; 10:1–2; 58:6–7; Jeremiah 7:5–7; Amos 4:1; 8:4–6; Zechariah 7:9–10; Malachi 3:5.
2. Donin, *To Be a Jew*, 48–52.
3. Turner, *Islam*, 152–56.
4. The exact quotation is, "Seeking the face of God in everything, everyone, all the time, and his hand in every happening; this is what it means to be contemplative in the heart of the world. Seeing and adoring the presence of Jesus, especially in the lowly appearance of bread, and in the distressing disguise of the poor" (Mother Teresa, *In the Heart of the World*, 33).
5. Holland, *Christ and the New Covenant*, 336–37.
6. *Century Hymnal*, no. 164, p. 128.
7. Wilberg, *Love Divine, All Loves Excelling.*

SOURCES

Alexander's Hymns No. 4. Edited by Charles M. Alexander and Edwin H. Bookmyer. Philadelphia: Sterling Music Company, 1921.

Al-Ghazālī, Abū Hāmid Muḥammad. *Inner Dimensions of Islamic Worship.* Translated by Muhtar Holland. Markfield, Leicestershire: Islamic Foundation, 1983.

Allen, James B., and Glen M. Leonard. *The Story of the Latter-day Saints.* Rev. ed. Salt Lake City: Deseret Book, 1992.

Anchor Bible Dictionary. Edited by David Noel Freedman. 6 vols. New York: Doubleday, 1992.

Anderson, Devery S., and Gary James Bergera. *Joseph Smith's Quorum of the Anointed: A Documentary History.* Salt Lake City: Signature Books, 2005.

The Apostolic Fathers: Greek Texts and English Translations. Edited and translated by Michael W. Holmes. 3d ed. Grand Rapids, Mich.: Baker Academic, 2007.

Armstrong, Karen. *Jerusalem: One City, Three Faiths.* New York: Ballantine Books, 1997.

Augustine. *Expositions of the Psalms.* Translated by Maria Boulding. The Works of St. Augustine: A Translation for the 21st Century. 6 vols. Hyde Park, N.Y.: New City Press, 2001.

Ballard, M. Russell. "Pure Testimony." *Ensign,* November 2004, 40–42.

SOURCES

Bandstra, Barry L. *Reading the Old Testament.* Belmont, Calif.: Wadsworth, 2004.

The Baptist Hymn Book. Edited by Gilbert Beebe. 2d stereotype ed. Middleton, N.Y.: Signs of the Times, 1859.

Barlow, Philip L. *Mormons and the Bible: The Place of Latter-day Saints in American Religion.* New York: Oxford University Press, 1991.

Barrett, Ivan J. *Joseph Smith and the Restoration.* Provo, Utah: Brigham Young University Press, 1973.

Bauer, Walter. *A Greek-English Lexicon of the New Testament.* Edited by Frederick William Danker. 3d ed. Chicago: University of Chicago Press, 2000.

Bednar, David A. "A Reservoir of Living Water." Brigham Young University fireside, February 4, 2007, speeches.byu.edu.

———. "Honorably Hold a Name and Standing." *Ensign,* May 2009, 97–100.

———. "More Diligent and Concerned at Home." *Ensign,* November 2009, 17–20.

———. "Pray Always." *Ensign,* November 2008, 41–44.

Belnap, Daniel L., ed. *By Our Rites of Worship: Latter-day Saint Views on Ritual in Scripture, History, and Practice.* Provo, Utah: Brigham Young University, Religious Studies Center, 2013.

Benson, Ezra Taft. "The Book of Mormon and the Doctrine and Covenants." *Ensign,* May 1987, 83–85.

Block, Daniel I. *For the Glory of God: Recovering a Biblical Theology of Worship.* Grand Rapids, Mich.: Baker Academic, 2014.

Bokovoy, David E. *Authoring the Old Testament: Genesis–Deuteronomy.* Salt Lake City: Kofford Books, 2004.

Brown, Francis, S. R. Driver, and C. Briggs. *The Brown-Driver-Briggs Hebrew and English Lexicon.* Peabody, Mass.: Hendrickson, 1906. Reprint, 2008.

Brown, Raymond E. *The Gospel according to John.* Vol. 29 of Anchor Bible. New York: Doubleday, 1966.

Brown, Samuel M. *First Principles and Ordinances.* Provo, Utah: Neal A. Maxwell Institute for Religious Scholarship, 2014.

Brueggemann, Walter. *Worship in Ancient Israel: An Essential Guide.* Nashville, Tenn.: Abingdon Press, 2005.

Bushman, Richard L. *Joseph Smith, Rough Stone Rolling.* New York: Vintage, 2005.

SOURCES

Cannon, Jon. *The Secret Language of Sacred Places: Decoding Churches, Temples, Mosques, and Other Places of Worship around the World*. London: Duncan Baird Publishers, 2013.

The Catholic Encyclopedia. Edited by Robert C. Broderick. Nashville, Tenn.: T. Nelson, 1913.

The Century Hymnal. Edited by H. Augustine Smith. New York: Century, 1921.

Chappell, Bryan. *Christ-Centered Worship*. Grand Rapids, Mich.: Baker Academic, 2009.

Children's Songbook. Salt Lake City: The Church of Jesus Christ of Latter-day Saints, 1995.

"Church Leaders Call for Better Observance of Sabbath Day." Church Newsroom, June 30, 2015. Accessed July 25, 2015, http://www.mormonnewsroom.org/article/church-leaders-call-for-better-observance-of-sabbath-day.

deClaissé-Walford, Nancy, Rolf A. Jacobson, and Beth LaNeel Tanner. *The Book of Psalms*. The New International Commentary on the Old Testament. Grand Rapids, Mich.: Eerdmans, 2014.

Discourses of Brigham Young. Edited by John A. Widtsoe. Salt Lake City: Deseret Book, 1978.

Documents, February 1833–March 1834. Edited by Gerrit J. Dirkmaat, Brent M. Rogers, Grant Underwood, Robert J. Woodford, and William G. Hartley. Vol. 3 of Documents series of The Joseph Smith Papers, edited by Ronald K. Esplin and Matthew J. Grow. Salt Lake City: Church Historian's Press, 2014.

Donin, Hayim Halevy. *To Be a Jew: A Guide to Observance in Contemporary Life*. New York: BasicBooks, 1972.

———. *To Pray as a Jew: A Guide to the Prayer Book and the Synagogue Service*. New York: BasicBooks, 1980.

Dudley, Martin, and Geoffrey Rowell, eds. *The Oil of Gladness: Anointing in the Christian Tradition*. Collegeville, Minn.: Liturgical Press, 1993.

Eerdmans Dictionary of the Bible. Edited by David Noel Freedman. Grand Rapids, Mich.: Eerdmans, 2000.

Encyclopedia of Mormonism. Edited by Daniel H. Ludlow. 4 vols. New York: Macmillan, 1992.

Evans, Craig A. *Fabricating Jesus: How Modern Scholars Distort the Gospels*. Downers Grove, Ill.: InterVarsity Press, 2006.

Exegetical Dictionary of the New Testament. Edited by Horst Balz and Gerhard Schneider. 3 vols. Grand Rapids, Mich.: Eerdmans, 1990–93.

Eyring, Henry B. "Exhort Them to Pray." *Ensign*, February 2012, 4.

———. "The Prayer of Faith." *Ensign*, October 2014, 4–5.

Farley, Lawrence R. *Following Egeria: A Visit to the Holy Land through Time and Space.* Chesterton, Ind.: Ancient Faith Publishing, 2014.

"Father, Consider Your Ways." *Ensign*, June 2002, 12–16.

Fleming, Daniel. "The Biblical Tradition of Anointing Priests." *Journal of Biblical Literature* 117, no. 3 (1998): 401–14.

France, R. T. *The Gospel of Matthew.* International Commentary on the New Testament. Grand Rapids, Mich.: Eerdmans, 2007.

Frishman, Martin, and Hasan-uddin Khan. *The Mosque.* London: Thames & Hudson, 1994.

Gunaratana, Henepola. *Mindfulness in Plain English.* Boston: Wisdom Publications, 1994.

Hales, Robert C. "Holy Scriptures: The Power of God unto Our Salvation." *Ensign*, November 2006, 24–27.

Harper, Steven C. *Joseph Smith's First Vision: A Guide to the Historical Accounts.* Salt Lake City: Deseret Book, 2012.

Hatch, Verena Ursenbach. *Worship and Music in The Church of Jesus Christ of Latter-day Saints.* Provo, Utah: M. Ephraim Hatch, 1968.

Hess, Richard S. *Israelite Religions: An Archaeological and Biblical Survey.* Grand Rapids, Mich.: BakerAcademic, 2007.

Hicks, Michael. *Mormonism and Music: A History.* Urbana: University of Illinois Press, 2003.

———. *The Tabernacle Choir: A Biography.* Urbana: University of Illinois Press, 2015.

Hill, E. Jeffrey. "Five Ways to Celebrate the Sabbath as a Family." *Church News and Events.* July 20, 2015. Acessed July 25, 2015, https://www.lds.org/church/news/print/five-ways-to-celebrate-the-sabbath-as-a-family?lang=eng.

Hinckley, Gordon B. "The Father, Son, and Holy Ghost." *Ensign*, November 1986, 49–51.

———. "The Stone Cut Out of the Mountain." *Ensign*, October 2007, 83–86.

———. "The Wondrous and True Story of Christmas." *Ensign*, December 2002, 2–6.

Histories, 1832–1844. Edited by Karen Lynn Davidson, David J. Whittaker,

Mark Ashurst-Gee, and Richard L. Jensen. Vol. 1 of Histories series of The Joseph Smith Papers, edited by Dean C. Jessee, Ronald K. Esplin, and Richard Lyman Bushman. Salt Lake City: Church Historian's Press, 2012.

History of The Church of Jesus Christ of Latter-day Saints. Edited by B. H. Roberts. 7 vols. 2d ed. rev. Salt Lake City: The Church of Jesus Christ of Latter-day Saints, 1932–51.

Holland, Jeffrey R. *Christ and the New Covenant: The Messianic Message of the Book of Mormon.* Salt Lake City: Deseret Book, 1997.

———. "This Do in Remembrance of Me." *Ensign*, November 1995, 67–69.

———. "Where Justice, Love, and Mercy Meet." *Ensign*, May 2015, 104–6.

Holzapfel, Richard Neitzel, Eric D. Huntsman, and Thomas A. Wayment. *Jesus Christ and the World of the New Testament.* Salt Lake City: Deseret Book, 2006.

Holzapfel, Richard Neitzel, Dana Pike, and David Seely. *Jehovah and the World of the Old Testament.* Salt Lake City: Deseret Book, 2009.

Holzapfel, Richard Neitzel, and Thomas A. Wayment. *From the Last Supper through the Resurrection: The Savior's Final Hours.* Salt Lake City: Deseret Book, 2003.

Huntington, Ray L., David M. Whitchurch, and Frank F. Judd, eds. *The New Testament Brought to Light: Latter-day Saint Insights into Acts through Revelation.* Provo, Utah: Brigham Young University, Religious Studies Center, 2009.

Huntsman, Eric D. "'And the Word Was Made Flesh': A Latter-day Saint Exegesis of the Blood and Water Imagery in the Gospel of John." *Studies in the Bible and Antiquity* 1 (2009): 51–65.

———. *God So Loved the World: The Final Days of the Savior's Life.* Salt Lake City: Deseret Book, 2011.

———. *Good Tidings of Great Joy: An Advent Celebration of the Savior's Birth.* Salt Lake City: Deseret Book, 2011.

———. *The Miracles of Jesus.* Salt Lake City: Deseret Book, 2014.

Hye, Abdul. *Basics of Islam.* CreateSpace Independent Publishing Platform, 1999.

Hymns of The Church of Jesus Christ of Latter-day Saints. Salt Lake City: The Church of Jesus Christ of Latter-day Saints, 1985.

SOURCES

Jackson, Kent P., ed. *How the New Testament Came to Be.* Salt Lake City: Deseret Book, 2006.

———. *The King James Bible and the Restoration.* Salt Lake City: Deseret Book, 2011.

Jackson, Kent P., and Robert L. Millet, eds. *Genesis to 2 Samuel.* Vol. 3 of Studies in Scripture series. Salt Lake City: Deseret Book, 1989.

Jeremias, Joachim. *The Prayers of Jesus.* Studies in Biblical Theology Second Series 6. London: SCM Press, 1967.

Jessop, Craig D. "Music and Mormons." *Mormon Identities,* episode 66. Mormon Channel. 2011. Accessed July 29, 2015, http://www.mormonchannel.org/listen/series/mormon-identities-audio/music-and-mormons-episode-66.

Josephus. *Antiquities of the Jews* and *Wars of the Jews.* In *The Complete Works of Josephus.* Edited by Paul L. Maier. Translated by William Whiston. Rev. ed. Grand Rapids: Mich.: Kregel, 1999.

Journal of Discourses. 26 vols. London: Latter-day Saints' Book Depot, 1854–86.

Journals, 1832–1839. Edited by Dean C. Jessee, Mark Ashurst-McGee, and Richard L. Jensen. Vol. 1 of Journals series of The Joseph Smith Papers, edited by Dean C. Jessee, Ronald K. Esplin, and Richard Lyman Bushman. Salt Lake City: Church Historian's Press, 2008.

Journals, May 1843–June 1844. Edited by Andrew Hedges, Alex D. Smith, and Brent M. Rogers. Vol. 3 of Journals series of The Joseph Smith Papers, edited by Ronald K. Esplin and Matthew J. Grow. Salt Lake City: Church Historian's Press, 2015.

Judd, Frank F., Jr., Eric D. Huntsman, and Shon D. Hopkin. *The Ministry of Peter, the Chief Apostle.* Sidney B. Sperry Symposium series. Provo, Utah: Brigham Young University, Religious Studies Center, 2014.

Kierkegaard, Søren. *Purity of Heart Is to Will One Thing: Spiritual Preparation for the Feast of Confession.* Translated by Douglas V. Steere. New York: Harper and Brothers, 1938.

Kimball, Spencer W. *Faith Precedes the Miracle.* Salt Lake City: Deseret Book, 1972.

———. "The Sabbath—A Delight." *Ensign,* January 1978, 2–5.

Kraus, Hans-Joachim. *Worship in Israel.* Translated by Geoffrey Buswell. Oxford: Basil Blackwell, 1965.

SOURCES

Landau, Yehezkel. "An Interview with Krister Stendahl." *Harvard Divinity Bulletin* 35, no. 1 (Winter 2007): 29–31.

Lane, George. *Christian Spirituality: A Historical Sketch*. Chicago: Loyola, 1984.

Marcus, Ivan. *Rituals of Childhood: Jewish Acculturation in Medieval Europe*. New Haven, Conn.: Yale University Press, 1996.

Marriott, Neill F. "Yielding Our Hearts to God." *Ensign*, November 2015, 30–32.

Martin, Douglas. "Krister Stendahl, 86, Ecumenical Bishop, Is Dead." *New York Times*, April 16, 2008. Accessed August 18, 2015, http://www.nytimes.com/2008/04/16/us/16stendahl.html.

Maurer, John A. "Music in the World of Islam: handasah al sawt." Accessed July 31, 2015, https://ccrma.stanford.edu/~blackrse/islam.html#references.

McConkie, Bruce R. "How to Worship." *Ensign*, December 1971, 129–30.

———. "The Lord God of the Restoration." *Ensign*, November 1980, 50–52.

Millet, Robert L., Camille Fronk Olson, Andrew C. Skinner, and Brent L. Top. *LDS Beliefs: A Doctrinal Reference*. Salt Lake City: Deseret Book, 2011.

Millgram, Abraham. *Jewish Worship*. Philadelphia: Jewish Publication Society of America, 1971.

Mouw, Richard J., and Mark A. Noll, eds. *Wonderful Words of Life: Hymns in American Protestant History and Theology*. Grand Rapids, Mich.: Eerdmans, 2004.

Neiger, Brad L. "To Act in Holiness before the Lord." Brigham Young University fireside, April 4, 2006. speeches.byu.edu.

Nelson, Russell M. "The Sabbath Is a Delight." *Ensign*, May 2015, 129–32.

Neuenschwander, Dennis B. "Ordinances and Covenants." *Ensign*, August 2001, 20–26.

New Catholic Encyclopedia. New York: McGraw Hill, 1967.

Nibley, Hugh. *Temple and Cosmos: Beyond This Ignorant Present*. Vol. 12 of Collected Works of Hugh Nibley. Salt Lake City: Deseret Book, 1992.

Nolland, John. *The Gospel of Matthew*. The New International Greek Testament Commentary. Grand Rapids, Mich.: Eerdmans, 2005.

Oaks, Dallin H. "The Keys and Authority of the Priesthood." *Ensign*, May 2014, 49–52.

———. "The Language of Prayer." *Ensign*, May 1993, 15–18.

———. *In His Holy Name*. Salt Lake City: Deseret Book, 1998.

Oxford Dictionary of English Etymology. Edited by C. T. Onions. Oxford: Oxford University Press, 1966.

Oxford Latin Dictionary. Edited by P. G. W. Glare. Oxford: Clarendon Press, 1982.

Packer, Boyd K. "The Gift of the Holy Ghost: What Every Member Should Know." *Ensign*, August 2006, 46–52.

———. "Inspiring Music—Worthy Thoughts." *Ensign*, November 1973, 21–23.

———. "Reverence Invites Revelation." *Ensign*, November 1991, 21–23.

Petersen, Mark E. "The Sabbath Day." *Ensign*, May 1975, 47–49.

Peterson, David. *Engaging with God: A Biblical Theology of Worship*. Downers Grove, Ill.: IVP Academic, 1992.

Philo. *The Works of Philo*. Translated by C. D. Yonge. Peabody, Mass.: Hendrickson, 1993.

Plewe, Brandon S. *Mapping Mormonism*. 2d ed. Provo, Utah: BYU Studies, 2014.

Prayer. Salt Lake City: Deseret Book, 1977.

Preach My Gospel: A Guide to Missionary Service. Salt Lake City: The Church of Jesus Christ of Latter-day Saints, 2004.

"*The Redeemer* Performed for Easter: Tabernacle Choir, Orchestra Present Robert Cundick's Sacred Masterwork." *Church News*, March 29, 2008.

Rojas, Jorge A. "Covenants and Ordinances." *Ensign*, October 1991, 44–45.

Runes, Dagobert D. *Dictionary of Philosophy*. Rev. ed. Savage, Md.: Adams Littlefield, 1983.

Seely, David Rolph, and Jeffrey R. Chadwick, eds. *Ascending the Mountain of the Lord*. Provo, Utah: Brigham Young University, Religious Studies Center, 2013.

Shalev-Hurvitz, Vered. *Holy Sites Encircled: The Early Byzantine Concentric Churches of Jerusalem*. Oxford: Oxford University Press, 2015.

Shiloah, Amnon. *Music in the World of Islam: A Socio-Cultural Study*. London: Scholars Press, 1995.

Skinner, Andrew C. *Temple Worship: 20 Truths That Will Bless Your Life*. Salt Lake City: Deseret Book, 2007.

SOURCES

Smith, Joseph. *Joseph Smith*. Teachings of Presidents of the Church series. Salt Lake City: The Church of Jesus Christ of Latter-day Saints, 2007.

———. *Teachings of the Prophet Joseph Smith*. Selected by Joseph Fielding Smith. Salt Lake City: Deseret Book, 1976.

Smith, Joseph Fielding. *Doctrines of Salvation*. Comp. Bruce R. McConkie. 3 vols. Salt Lake City: Bookcraft, 1954–56.

Smith, Lucy Mack. *The Revised and Enhanced History of Joseph Smith by His Mother*. Edited by Scot Facer Proctor and Maurine Jensen Proctor. Salt Lake City: Bookcraft, 1996.

The Stanford Encyclopedia of Philosophy. Edited by Edward N. Zalta. Accessed January 31, 2015, http://plato.stanford.edu/archives/win2014/entries/intentionality.

Teresa, Mother. *In the Heart of the World: Thoughts, Stories and Prayers*. Novato, Calif.: New World Library, 2010.

Theological Dictionary of the New Testament. Edited by Gerhard Kittel. Translated by Gerhard Friedrich and Geoffrey William Bromiley. 10 vols. Grand Rapids, Mich.: Eerdmans, 1984.

Theological Dictionary of the Old Testament. Edited by G. Johannes Botterweck, Helmer Ringgren, and Heinz-Josef Fabry. Translated by David E. Green, Douglas W. Stott, and John T. Willis. 15 vols. Grand Rapids, Mich.: Eerdmans, 1974–2006.

Thompson, Marjorie J., and Evan B. Howard. *Soul Feast: An Invitation to the Christian Spiritual Life*. Grand Rapids, Mich.: Westminster John Knox Press, 1995.

Tozer, A. W. *The Purpose of Man: Designed to Worship*. Edited by James L. Snyder. Ventura, Calif.: Regal, 2009.

Turner, Colin. *Islam: The Basics*. New York: Routledge, 2011.

Uchtdorf, Dieter F. "The Gift of Grace." *Ensign*, May 2015, 107–10.

Van Vreeswijk, Michiel, Jenny Broersen, and Ger Schurink. *Mindfulness*. London: Wiley-Blackwell, 2014.

"Vår Och Andras Tro." Mormon Lady Blog. August 4, 2011. Accessed October 7, 2015, http://mormonlady.se/2011/08/04/var-och-andras-tro/.

Von Dehsen, Christian D. "Hymnic Forms in the New Testament." *Reformed Liturgy and Music* 18, no. 1 (Winter 1984): 7–11.

Vulliamy, Ed. "Let's Roll: The Real Story of Flight 93." *The Guardian*,

December 1, 2001. Accessed January 17, 2015, http://www.theguardian.com/world/2001/dec/02/september11.terrorism1.

Wainwright, Geoffrey, and Karen B. Westerfield Tucker, eds. *The Oxford History of Christian Worship*, edited by Oxford: Oxford University Press, 2006.

Wayment, Thomas A., and Keith J. Wilson, eds. *Celebrating Easter*. Provo, Utah: Brigham Young University, Religious Studies Center, 2006.

Webber, Robert E. *Worship, Old and New*. Rev. ed. Grand Rapids, Mich.: Zondervan, 1994.

The Westminster Hymnal for Congregational and Social Use and for the Sunday School. Philadelphia: Presbyterian Board of Publication and Sabbath School Work, 1911.

White, James F. *A Brief History of Christian Worship*. Nashville, Tenn.: Abingdon, 1993.

———. *Introduction to Christian Worship*. 3d ed. rev. Nashville, Tenn.: Abingdon Press, 2000.

Wilberg, Mack. *Come, Ye Thankful People, Come*. Oxford: Oxford University Press, 2006.

———. "His Voice as the Sound." In *My Song in the Night*. Oxford: Oxford University Press, 2009.

———. *Love Divine, All Loves Excelling*. Oxford: Oxford University Press, 2002.

Wirthlin, Joseph B. "Pulling in the Gospel Net." *Ensign*, November 1986, 59–61.

Wolff, Christoph. *Johann Sebastian Bach: The Learned Musician*. New York: Norton, 2013.

Zaleski, Philip, and Carol Zaleski. *Prayer: A History*. Boston: Houghton, 2006.

INDEX

"A Mighty Fortress Is Our God," 123
Aaronic Priesthood, 50
Abraham, 9, 58–59
Adam and Eve: worship of, 2; prayers of, 16; know gospel plan, 37; in Garden of Eden, 56; at Adam-ondi-Ahman, 58
Adhān (call to prayer), 22, 123
Adoration, 2
Advent, 86, 87
Al-Aqsa Mosque, 22, 64
Alford, Henry, 125
Al-Ghazālī, Abū Ḥāmid Muḥammad, 25
Allāh (God), 24
Alma, 33
Almsgiving, 135
Altars, 58, 150n8
Ambrose of Milan, 122
Amulek (Book of Mormon), 31, 33
Anna (New Testament), 58
Anointings: Old Testament, 38, 44, 116; New Testament, 44; of Jesus, 100, 115; in the Restoration, 53
Antiphonal singing, 122
Apostles, early, 43–44, 101–2
Apostolic period, 101
Ashton, Marvin J., 30
Assembly Hall, 70
Atonement, 32, 36, 50, 54, 58–59, 71, 79–80, 117
Augustine of Hippo, 122
Authority. *See* Priesthood authority

Bach, Johann Sebastian, 123–24, 125
Baden, Austria, 61
Ballard, M. Russell, 110
Bandstra, Barry, 116
Baptism: personal experience of, 39–40, 48; as worship, 40–41; of Jesus, 35, 40–42, 142n15; symbolism of, 41; in the New Testament, 41–43; as practiced by postapostolic Christianity, 45–46, 47–48, 147n40; as saving ordinance, 49, 60;

INDEX

in restored gospel, 34, 50–51, 87, 93, 148n54; vicarious, for the dead, 68, 71, 152n44
Baptizō (dip, immerse) 40
Basilica of the Nativity, 66
Basilicas, 65
Battalogeō (speak repetitiously), 20
Beamer, Todd, 18
Bednar, David R., 92, 109
Benedict of Nursia, Saint, 105
Benedictus, 117
Benjamin, King, 134–35
Benson, Ezra Taft, 108
Bêṯ HaMiqdāš (the holy house), 57
Bethel, 59
Bible, King James Version, 30–31, 107. *See also* New Testament, Old Testament, Scriptures
Bishoprics, role in fostering worship, 88, 91, 110, 129
"Bless Our Fast, We Pray," 90–91
Blessings, 32, 38, 46, 52, 71, 84, 112, 127; of Adam's posterity, 58; of John the Baptist, 117; other Jewish blessings, 84–85, 96; on meals, 24, 45; priesthood blessings, 43, 49, 52–53, 74; in postapostolic Christianity, 46; of author's mother, 74
Block, Daniel, 82, 115
Book of Commandments, 107
Book of Mormon, 31, 107. *See also* Scriptures
Bread of Life discourse, 43, 80–81
Brigham Young University–Jerusalem Center, 11, 22, 37, 64, 83, 96

Calvinists, 124
Camp meetings, 126
Canticles (songs), 26, 117, 157n14
Cantor, 122
Cathedral prayers, 24
Cemeteries, 55
Change. *See* Transformation, personal
Chapels, 70
Chappell, Bryan, 95
Charis (grace), 46
Charity, 135–36
Chichester Psalms, 113–14
Children, 30
Children's Songbook, 130
Choirs, 129
"Christ the Lord Is Risen Today," 124
Christians, early: prayers of, 23–24; rituals of, 45, 151n24; worship services of, 62–63, 143n30; observe the Sabbath, 81–82; canticles of, 117–18; music of, 122
Christmas: as sacred time, 76, 85, 86, 90; highlight scriptures during, 110; music celebrating, 130–31
Christological hymns, 119
Chronicler, the, 99
Chronos (flow of time), 75
Chrysostom, John, 104
Church of Jesus Christ of Latter-day Saints, The: establishment of, 50–51, 68; sacred places of, 69–74; establishes Sabbath worship, 87–88; and fasting, 90; celebrates Christmas and Easter, 91; music of, 128–31; rebaptism within, 148n54. *See also* Restoration
Church of the Holy Sepulchre, 64, 66
Clothing, sacred, 35, 38, 53, 59
Collection of Sacred Hymns for the Church of the Latter Day Saints, A, 127
"Come, Redeemer of the Nations," 122
"Come, We That Love the Lord," 124

INDEX

"Come, Ye Thankful People, Come," 125
Communal prayers, 23, 86
Communion, 44, 51
Community of faith: built by ordinances, 35; united by baptism, 42; united by the sacrament, 51; united in places of worship, 63; united on Sabbath, 88; united by music, 128
Confirmation: in the New Testament, 43–44, 146n32; in other faiths, 46, 47; within restored gospel, 50–51
Consistency, 92
Covenants: connected to ordinances, 36; of baptism, 41, 50; of sacrament, 42–43, 51–52; in temple, 71–72; taught through scriptures, 97
Cowdery, Oliver, 50, 53
Creation, 78, 79, 82, 149–50n2
Cundick, Robert, 117

Daniel (Old Testament), 17
Daniel, book of, 99
David (Old Testament), 115–16
Day of Atonement, 60, 79–80
Deseret Sunday School Union Music Book, 127
Divine reading, 105, 109
Doctrine and Covenants, 107–8
Documentary Hypothesis, 154–55n4
Donin, Hayim Halevy, Rabbi, 8, 16, 78
Duʻāʼ (supplication), 25

Easter: as sacred time, 76, 85, 91–92; highlight scriptures during, 110; music celebrating, 130–31; in KJV, 153n24
Ecclesiastes, 98
Egeria, 153–54

Elias (Old Testament), 53
Elijah (Old Testament), 3
Elohim (God), 24
Endowment. *See* Ordinances, temple ceremonies
Endowment House, 152n44
Envy, holy, 11, 12, 132
Epoiēsen (appoint), 43
Esther, book of, 99
Euangellion, 101
Eucharist, 46, 51, 85, 104
Eucharistia (thanksgiving), 46
Exalting ordinances, 49, 53–54, 71–72
Eyring, Henry B., 13, 32
Ezekiel (Old Testament), 94
Ezra (Old Testament), 99, 141n9

Fall, the, 6, 16, 34, 53, 56, 58
Family. *See* Homes
Family prayer, 26, 32
Fast of Tisha b'Av, 84
Fasting: in the Old Testament, 18; Muslim; 25, 86, 90; personal experiences with, 26; in the New Testament, 58; in the Restoration, 70, 80, 86, 90–91, 140n17; Jewish, 80, 84, 86
Father, God as, 20, 30
Fear of the Lord, 1, 7, 133
Feast of Tabernacles, 79
Feasting on word of God, 94–95
Festival of Weeks, 79
Festivals, 79–80
First Vision, 27–28, 30, 108
Five Pillars of Islam, 24–25, 66, 86, 135
Focusing, as component of worship, 3, 7–9, 12, 14, 29–30
Forgiveness, 21, 40
Funerals, 110–11

INDEX

Garden of Eden, 56, 60
Gloria in excelsis, 117
God: reasons for worshipping, 2–3; worshipping with focus, 7–9, 29–30; being in presence of, 17, 57; as Father, 20; following will of, 32–33
Gospel, 101. *See also* Church of Jesus Christ of Latter-day Saints
Gospel plan, 37
Grace, 5, 25, 34, 44, 46; of Jesus Christ, 3, 11, 33, 40, 54, 71
Grant, Heber J., 127
Gratitude, 79
Gregorian chant, 122
Gregory the Great, 86
Group prayer, 29, 32

Ḥagg (pilgrimage), 66
Halākāh (legal writings), 97
Hales, Robert D., 110
Hallel Psalms, 118–19, 157n13
handasah al ṣawt (art of sound), 123
Handel, George Frideric, 120, 124, 125
Hannah (Old Testament), 17–18, 58; Song of, 114–15
Ḥarām al-Sharīf (Temple Mount), 22, 105
Harmony, 125
Hasidic Tzanzer Rebbe, 141n4
Hatch, Verena Ursenbach, 113, 140n17
Haydn, Franz Josef, 129
Ḥazzān (cantor), 122
"He Died! The Great Redeemer Died," 124
Healings, 44, 46, 52, 81, 147n33
Heaven, 56
Hebrew Bible, 96–100
Hebrew language, 23, 142–43n26
He-Hasid, Judah, rabbi, 121

Ḥesed (loving kindness), 45, 135
Hezekiah, king, 116
Hinckley, Gordon B., 30, 87, 140n11
"His Voice as the Sound of a Dulcimer Sweet," 3, 139n6
Historical sites, 55
Holiness, 60, 141n20
Holland, Jeffrey R., 42–43, 149–50n2
Holy Ghost: gift of, 50–51, 146–47n32; sanctifying power of, 51, 76; gifts of, 52;
Holy of Holies, 60
Holy Place, 60
Holy Week, 83, 85, 86–87
Homes: as sacred places, 55, 60, 65, 73–74; celebrating Easter in, 85, 92; celebrating Christmas in, 91; music and worship in, 122
Homothymadon (one accord), 21
House churches, 62, 151n24
Huntsman, Marilyn (author's mother), 9, 57–58, 74, 110; music and, 117
Huntsman, Dennis C. (author's father), 9, 57, 78
Huntsman, Elaine (author's wife), 73, 77, 80
Huntsman, Rachel (author's daughter), 39–40, 74, 80, 83, 105
Huntsman, Samuel (author's son), 26–27, 48–49
Ḥwh (prostration), 4
Hymnody, 122
Hymns of The Church of Jesus Christ of Latter-day Saints, 127–28
Hymns, of LDS Church, 127–31
Hypokritai (play actors), 20

"I Love to See the Temple," 67–68
Imām (prayer leader), 47, 67, 86
Infant baptism, 46, 48, 50, 147n40

INDEX

Intentionality: of worship, 7–9, 12, 133; of prayer, 16–17, 20, 28–30; in ordinance participation, 25, 39, 40; within Law of Moses, 38; of rituals in other faiths, 44–48; of temple worship, 72–73; in times of worship, 92–93; in scripture study, 95, 108–10; of worship through music, 128–29

Isaac (Old Testament), 58–59

Islamic worship: prayer in, 22–23, 24–25, 86, 151n31; meaning of, 24; ritual practices of, 47; pilgrimages in, 66; and Ramaḍān, 86; sacred book of, 105; music of, 123; as natural, 132; service within, 135; and obedience, 143n33

Israelites, 37–39, 77–79, 97

Jacob (Book of Mormon), 31, 59
James (New Testament), 50
Jefferson, Lisa, 18
Jehovah, 80, 97. *See also* YHWH
Jeremiah (Old Testament), 94
Jerusalem, 11, 64, 85
Jerusalem Council, 81
Jerusalem, heavenly, 111
Jerusalem Temple, 57, 60, 64, 79, 121, 129, 135
Jessop, Craig, 112–13, 126
Jesus Christ: on how to worship, 4; worshipping in name of, 6, 11; on manner of prayer, 19–21, 142n15; baptism of, 40–41; administers Last Supper, 42–43; acting in behalf of, 44; worships in synagogues and temples, 61–62; institutes work among the dead, 72; observes sacred times, 80–82; as focus of Sabbath worship, 89; is prophesied of, 98; teaches through scripture, 100–102; is central to apostolic proclamations, 101–2; early Christian songs about, 119–20; counsels Nicodemus, 133–34. *See also* Atonement

Jewish history, 97–99

Jewish worship: prayers in, 23–24; rituals of, 45, 150n12; in synagogues, 61–62, 65; in temples, 73; of the Sabbath, 77, 83; of festival days, 78–79, 83; Torah read in, 103; music in, 121–22; service within, 135

Job, book of, 98
John (New Testament), 50, 82, 120
John the Baptist, 40–41, 50
Joseph Smith Translation of Bible (JST), 70
"Joy to the World," 124
Jubal, 114
Jumu'ah (communal ritual prayer), 86
Junior Sunday School, story of, 7–8

Ka'ba, 66, 151n28
Kainē diathēkē (new covenant or testament), 43
Kairos (important moment), 75
Katangellō (proclaim), 43
Kavanah (proper intent): as focusing on God, 8, 14, 45, 73; in praying, 23; concentration with, 29; in scripture study, 95
Kērygma (testimony), 101, 155n17
Ketûbîm (Writings), 98–100
Kierkegaard, Søren, 15
Kimball, Spencer W., 78
Kirtland Temple, 53, 70
Kotel (Western Wall), 64–65

Language of prayer, 30–31, 144n52

INDEX

Last Supper, 46, 51, 118
Latter Day Saints' Psalmody, 127
Latter-day Saint Hymns, 127
Law of Moses: purpose of, 37–39; Sabbath as part of, 78, 81; establishes times of remembrance, 79; in Torah, 97; service as part of, 135
Laying on of hands: purposes of, 43–44; as saving ordinance, 49; as strengthening ordinance, 52; by apostles, 147n33
Lectio divina (divine reading), 105, 109
Liturgical hymns, 157n14
Liturgical year, 83, 85–86, 106
Longstaff, William D., 76, 82, 93
Lord's Prayer, 18–19, 20–21, 23, 142n19
Lord's Supper, 39, 40, 42–43, 45–46, 47, 49, 51, 62, 85, 87, 129
"Love Divine, All Love Excelling," 136–37
Luther, Martin, 25–26, 47, 86, 106, 123

Magnificat, 117, 118, 121
Marriage, 46
Marriott, Neill F., 52
Masjid (mosque), 66
McConkie, Bruce R., 16
Mecca, 66
Medina, 151n31
Meetinghouses, LDS, 68–69
Melchizedek Priesthood, 50, 148n57
Memorials, 66
Memory, role of, in worship, 35, 66, 75, 77, 87
Memphis Tennessee Temple, 57
Mendelssohn, Felix, 129
Messiah, 120, 124
Methodists, 124, 126

Mezuzah (parchment), 65
Middle Ages: prayer during, 24; illiteracy in, 104–5; music in, 117–18, 122–23; worship in, 143n30
Millgram, Abraham, 14, 141n20, 141n4
Mindfulness, 9–11, 39, 73, 95, 133–34; definition of, 140–41n19. *See also* Intentionality
Minyān (groups of Jewish men), 23
Miracles, 44
Mishnah, 156n22
Muḥammad, 47, 66, 151n31
Monastic communities, 105, 122
Montgomery, James, 14–15, 22, 25
Mormon Tabernacle Choir: role of, in LDS worship, 91, 117, 129–30; author sings with, 113–14, 125, 137
Moroni (Book of Mormon), 88, 108
Moses: teaches how to worship, 4; can't institute higher law, 37; restores sealing power, 53; and burning bush, 59; builds tabernacle in wilderness, 60; writings of, 96–97; as a type of Christ, 97; sings praises, 114
Mosques, 66–67
Mother Teresa, 135, 159n4
Mountaintops, 56–57
Mozart, Amadeus, 125
Mount Sinai, 59, 60
Music and the Spoken Word, 130
Music: worship through, 112–13; in Old Testament, 113–17; in New Testament, 117–20; early Christian music of, 122; in other faiths, 122–23
Muslims. *See* Islamic worship
Mystēria, 46
Mysteries, 46

INDEX

Nābī' (spokesperson), 98
Naos (temple), 56
Natural settings, 55
Nauvoo Temple, 70
Ne'ot Kedumim (Landscape Park), 96
Nebi'im (the Prophets), 98–100
Nelson, Russell M., 89–90
Nephi (Book of Mormon), 31
New Testament: places of worship in, 61; as scripture, 100–102; music references in, 117–21
Nibley, Hugh, 56
Niyyah (real intent), 25, 47
Nunc dimittis, 117, 118, 121
Nusah (musical prayers), 121–22

"O Thou, in Whose Presence My Soul Takes Delight," 139n6
Oaks, Dallin H., 30–31
Obedience, 5, 41
Offerings, 145n13. *See also* Sacrifices
Old Testament: prophets of, 58; temples of, 60; Sabbath worship in, 77–78; composition of, 97–99; music in, 114–17
Olsen, Bruce L., 32
Orchestra at Temple Square, 91, 117, 129
Ordinances: as type of worship, 34; definitions of, 35, 144n1; in other faiths, 47–48; restoration of, 49–54; within the temple, 49, 53–54, 70–72; vicarious, for the dead, 72–73, 152n44; explained by scriptures, 95; meaning of, 144n1
Ordination, in other faiths, 46

Packer, Boyd K.: on revelation, 6; on baptism and confirmation, 51; on worship in the chapel, 69–70; on Sabbath observance, 88; on music, 130, 158n41
Palestrina, Giovanni Pierluigi da, 124
Parents, heavenly, 15, 20, 30, 49, 54, 71, 133
Passover, 36, 79, 80, 118
Patriarchal blessings, 52
Paul (New Testament): on baptism, 40, 41, 42; on Last Supper, 42; on gifts of the Spirit, 52; on temple of God, 63; observes Sabbath, 81–82; preaches of Christ, 101; on worshipping through music, 118–19
Pearl of Great Price, 108
Peirasmon (test, trial), 21, 142n19
Penance, 46
Pentateuch, 97, 154–55n4
Perry, Janice Kapp, 67
Personal space, 6, 20, 28
Pesah (Passover), 79
Peter (New Testament), 50, 101
Peterson, David, 139n4
Peterson, Mark E., 88–89
Phelps, W. W., 127
Phobeomai (fear of the Lord), 7
Pilgrimages: Christian, 66, 85, 153–54n25; Islamic, 66; Israelite, 79
Pillars of Islam, 24–25, 66, 86, 135
Plainsong, 122
Poetry: in scripture, 96–98, 114–16, 117, 121, 157n14; Hebrew parallelism a feature of, 114–15; definition of, 115
Polyphony, 122–23, 124
Prayer: as communing, 13–14, 141n9; making, more meaningful, 15–17, 143n38; Christ teaches, 19–21; unity within, 21–23; within other religions, 23–26; in the Restoration, 26–33; language of, 30–31, 144n52;

INDEX

Latter-day Saint definition of, 32; expressed in music, 121–22
"Prayer Is the Soul's Sincere Desire," 14–15, 22, 25
Preparation, 28, 133
Priesthood authority, 36, 38, 43, 48–49, 53
Priesthood blessings, 49
Priesthood garments, 53, 68, 73, 150n13
Prophets, 98
Prophets, the (Hebrew Bible), 98–100, 103
Proskyneō (prostration), 4
Prostration, 4
Protestant Reformation: emphasizes prayer, 23, 25–26; rituals in, 47–48; and perception of sacred spaces, 67; limits Christian liturgical year, 86–87; communalizes scripture, 106; congregational singing in, 123–24
Proverbs, 98
Provo Utah Temple, 57–58
Psalm 119, 103–4
Psalmoi, 115
Psalms: prayers within, 17; express praise, 98; public reading of, 103; as music, 115–16, 121, 124, 157n8
Purification, 38
Puritans, 124

Qorbān (sacrifice), 38
Qur'ān, 105, 123

Rabbinic Judaism, 83–84, 140n15
Ramaḍān, 86, 105
Rector, Hartman, Jr., 30
Red brick store, Nauvoo, 70
Redeemer, The, 117

"Rejoice, the Lord Is King," 124
Religious art, 65–66
Religious buildings, 55
Religious orders, 24
Remission of sins, 50
Repetition, 20, 30
Restoration: Reformation sets pattern of prayer for, 26; and Joseph Smith's first prayer, 27–28; restores original ordinances, 48–54; holy places of, 67–71; and vicarious temple ordinances for the dead, 71–72; establishes Sabbath worship, 87–88; Book of Mormon pivotal to, 107; music of, 125–31
Revelation, 6, 48
Reverence: to prepare for worship, 6–7; to prepare for prayer, 28–29; in sacred places, 59, 69; for scriptures, 102–6
Rituals: as prayers of Muslims, 22, 24–25; of other faiths, 35, 44–48; of Law of Moses, 37–39; of laying on of hands, 43–44; of levels of holiness, 60–61
Roman Catholic traditions, 44, 46–47, 124–25, 143n30
Rosh Hashānāh, 79, 153n10
Ruth, book of, 99

Šābat (stop or cease), 78
Sabbath: as sacred time, 76–78; Jesus observes, 81–82; worshipping on, 89–90; music on, 130–31
Šābū'ōt (Festival of Weeks), 79
Sacrament: focusing on, 7–8; symbolism of, 39, 42, 59; as testament of believers, 43; example of, 48–49; within restored gospel,

INDEX

51; hymns for, 128; emblems of, 145n30
Sacrament meeting, 104, 110, 128, 156n33
Sacraments, in other faiths, 46–47
Sacred Harp, 126
Sacred spaces, 55
Sacred times, 75–76
Sacrifices, 38–39, 145n14, 150–51n17
Ṣalāt (Muslim ritual prayer), 22, 24–25, 47, 66, 86
Samuel (Old Testament), 18, 114–15
Sanctification, 51–52
Sanctuaries, 64
Saving ordinances, 49–51
Saviors on Mount Zion, 72
Scripture: as communication from God, 94; Old Testament as, 96–99; New Testament as, 100–102; valued in other faiths, 102–5; in Reformation, 106; in Restoration, 107–8; pondering and studying, 108–10; in LDS meetings, 156n33
Ṣedaqah (righteousness), 135
Seders, 37
Seeley, David, 40
September 11, 2001, 18
Sermon on the Mount, 101
Service, 134–35
"Service of the mind," 103
"Service of the word," 104
Sheheḥeyānû (blessing), 84–85
Shema, 139n7
Šḥḥ (prostration, worship), 4
Shul (school), 65
Sign of the cross, 24
Singing, congregational, 123, 126
Skinner, Andrew, 72, 73
Smith, Alvin, 71
Smith, Emma Hale, 53, 126

Smith, Joseph: on how to worship, 4; First Vision of, 27–28, 30; receives priesthood, 50; institutes temple ceremonies, 53; on temple building, 70–71; institutes vicarious temple ordinances, 71; from musical family, 126
Smith, Joseph F., 72
Smith, Joseph, Sr., 126
Smith, Lucy Mack, 126, 144n43
Southern Harmony, 126
Space for worship, 6–7, 8, 12, 133; in prayer, 14, 16, 17–18, 19, 25, 27, 28, 31; for ordinances, 35, 45, 51; and holy places, 55–56, 60, 63, 64, 66, 67, 69–70, 121, 150n13; and sacred time, 76, 78, 92; scripture helps create, 95, 109; music's role in creating, 113
Spirit, cannot force, 134
St. George Temple, 68
St. Mary's Episcopal Church, 83
Steere, Douglas V., 141n7
Stendahl, Krister, 11, 12, 132
Stockholm Sweden Temple, 11
Strengthening ordinances, 49, 52–53
Sukkôt (Festival of Tabernacles), 79
Sunnah, 47
Symbolism: within ordinances, 25, 49; of Law of Moses, 36–39; of baptism, 40–41; of sacrament, 42
Synagogues, 61–62, 65
Synoptic Gospels, 100

Tabernacles: Old Testament, 18, 53, 60, 70; pioneer-era, 62, 69; on Temple Square, 69, 129
"Take Time to Be Holy," 76, 82–83, 93
Talmud, 45, 156n22
Tameion (closet), 20

INDEX

Tanner, John S., 90
Tehillîm (songs of praise), 115
Temenos (sacred precinct), 56
Template, 56
Temple ceremonies, 49, 53–54, 70–73
Temple Mount, 22, 105
Temples, 56–57, 59–60, 70–74
Templum (temple), 56
Ten Commandments, 78, 97
Torah (teaching, instruction, law), 96–97, 99, 100, 103–4, 116, 154n4
Traditions, 85, 87
Transformation, personal: through worship, 3, 9–11, 136; through rituals, 39; through temple worship, 73–74; in sacred times, 93
Tullidge, John, 127

Uchtdorf, Dieter F., 5
United Airlines Flight 93, 18
Unity: of prayers, 21–22, 23; of baptism, 41; in sacred places, 63; through music, 128
Unsworth, Andrew E., 113

Veni redemptor gentium, 122

Waiting on the Lord, 15, 33–34
Ward councils, role in fostering worship, 88, 91, 104, 110

Washings, 38
Watt, Isaac, 124
Wesley, Charles, 124, 136
Wesley, John, 86, 124
Western Wall, 6, 64–65
Wilberg, Mack, 3, 125, 137, 139n6
Will of God, 32–33
Woodward, Ralph, 117
"Words of institution," 46, 51
Worship: meaning of, 2; outward expressions of, 4–5; creating space for, 6; focus and intentionality of, 7–9, 133; forms of, 11–12; arises from love of God, 132; service as, 135–36. *See also* Intentionality, Ordinances, Prayer, Sacrament, Sacred spaces, Sacred times, Scripture
Writings (of Hebrew Bible), 98–100, 103

Yardin, Ophir, 37
Yārē' (fear of the Lord), 7
YHWH, 80–81
Yôm Kippûr, 79–80
Young, Brigham, 71

Zakāt (almsgiving), 135
Zemîrôt (Sabbath songs), 122
Zwingli, Ulrich, 106, 124